The Hair Bun

By

Cosme Junior Chacon Segovia

Front Matter

For every soul who has felt the sting of exclusion, the hollow ache of silence, and the suffocating weight of fear in the echoing hallways of youth. This story is a tribute to the enduring grip of guilt, the dark tendrils of revenge, and the terrifying truth that some wounds never truly heal.

It is for those who understand that the most chilling monsters are often born from the shadows we cast ourselves, and that sometimes the past refuses to stay buried—clawing its way back into the present with a vengeance that knows no bounds. May this serve as a reminder that every action, no matter how small or seemingly insignificant, can unleash a storm, and that the consequences of cruelty can ripple far beyond our understanding, touching even the spectral realms.

For the Abigails of the world, whose stories were silenced too soon, and for the Hannahs who carry the unbearable weight of what was left undone. This is for the lingering dread that settles in the quiet moments, for the bumps in the night that feel too real, and for the chilling realization that sometimes the monsters are us—and sometimes, they are the vengeful spirits we create.

May you find solace in knowing you are not alone in the darkness, and that even in the most terrifying of tales lies a reflection of the struggles we all face, the choices we make, and the shadows that linger long after the lights go out.

This is for the courage it takes to confront our darkest selves—and for the hope, however faint, that redemption may still exist, even in the face of unspeakable horror.

Chapter 1:

The Shadow of Middle School

The fluorescent lights of Northwood Middle School hummed with a relentless, oppressive drone—a soundtrack to the perpetual motion of teenage life. Hallways painted a sterile, institutional beige stretched into infinity, teeming with a restless current of students. Each day was a carefully choreographed dance, a subtle negotiation of status and belonging. On the surface, Hannah moved with practiced grace. She was a girl of polite smiles and quiet nods, her voice rarely rising above a murmur, her presence as unobtrusive as a shadow. But beneath that carefully constructed façade of normalcy, a disquiet churned—a seed of unease planted by the unspoken rules that governed their world.

Her friends, Olivia, Emily, and Emma, formed a tight-knit constellation, their shared glances and knowing smiles a silent language only they understood. Olivia, with her sharp wit and sharper tongue, was the undisputed leader, her laughter loud and often at someone else's expense. Emily, ever the follower, mirrored Olivia's confidence, her loyalty a shield against potential threats. Emma, quieter and more observant, often acted as a bridge between Olivia's assertiveness and Hannah's reticence. Together, they navigated the treacherous social currents of Northwood—a unified front against the perceived dangers lurking beyond their circle. Hannah felt their collective pull, the unspoken expectation to conform, to participate, to be one of them. It was a comfortable, if suffocating, existence built on shared experiences and, as Hannah would soon discover, shared transgressions.

The school itself was a labyrinth of echoing lockers and crowded classrooms, a microcosm of adolescence where friendships blossomed and withered with equal speed. The lunchroom, a cacophony of scraping chairs and boisterous chatter, was a battleground of social maneuvering. Every table, every whispered conversation, every averted gaze spoke volumes, establishing the intricate, often brutal, pecking order that defined their days. Hannah watched it all with practiced detachment—part of the swirling mass, yet always a little outside it. She saw the subtle cruelties: whispered insults that clung to the air like static, pointed glares that could freeze a person in place. These were the undercurrents of Northwood, the festering cruelties beneath a veneer of normalcy. And Hannah, in her quiet way, began to feel the first tendrils of guilt coil within her.

It was in this swirling, indifferent atmosphere that Abigail existed—an anomaly in the vibrant tapestry of Northwood. She was a ghost before she became a memory, a girl who lived in the periphery, her presence overlooked, her voice lost in the din. Hannah's first real awareness of

Abigail came not through conversation but through the subtle shift in air whenever her name was mentioned—or, more often, when she was mocked. Abigail was the girl who read alone under the oak tree during lunch, her nose buried in a worn paperback. The one with perpetually smudged glasses and clothes that never quite fit. The one who always seemed on the verge of fading into the background.

The bullying began as a subtle art form, a series of nearly imperceptible jabs designed to chip away at her composure. Whispers loud enough to be overheard. Exclusion from group conversations. Hannah remembered one gray Tuesday, the air thick with the scent of damp leaves, when Olivia "accidentally" bumped Abigail in the hallway, sending her meticulously stacked notebooks scattering across the linoleum. Abigail scrambled to gather them, cheeks flushed crimson. Olivia offered a saccharine apology, her eyes twinkling with amusement devoid of remorse. Hannah, standing nearby with Emily and Emma, felt a knot twist in her stomach. She gave Abigail a weak, apologetic smile—an acknowledgment of the injustice—but did nothing more. The unspoken rule, the one that bound them together, demanded silence.

The cruelty escalated. Abigail's locker combination was changed, leading to her public humiliation when she couldn't open it. Anonymous, vicious messages appeared on her social media, each one a declaration of her worthlessness. Hannah knew, with bone-deep certainty, that these came from her friends. Her finger hovered over the delete button more than once, her mind a battlefield of conflicting impulses. But fear—of ostracization, of becoming the next target—kept her captive. Olivia's casual dismissal, *"She's asking for it, isn't she?"* echoed in her mind, twisting the knot tighter.

The motivations behind their cruelty were a tangled web of adolescent insecurity and the desperate need for dominance. Olivia craved the power of control. Emily, eager to please, masked her own fragility through obedience. Emma, quieter, was swept along by momentum, her hesitation drowned out by the group's will. And Hannah—polite, silent Hannah—hid her cowardice behind her passivity. Abigail, quiet and visibly vulnerable, became their scapegoat, the vessel for all their anxieties. The thrill of having a collective enemy, however twisted, pulled them deeper into a vortex of cruelty.

Hannah's carefully maintained politeness began to fray. Whispers became jeers. Abigail's sanctuary under the oak tree was invaded with laughter and insults. Hannah was caught between her growing discomfort and the pressure to remain loyal. She remembered one lunch period when Abigail walked past their table, shoulders hunched, backpack slipping from one arm. Olivia nudged Hannah. "Go on," she hissed. "Tell her that dress makes her look like a potato sack." Hannah froze, words stuck in her throat. She shook her head almost imperceptibly. Olivia's grin widened. "Fine," she announced, standing tall, her voice slicing through the lunchroom noise. "I'll do it myself."

The shame of that moment hollowed Hannah out. The cruelty was no longer subtle. It was systematic. Rumors spread, each more outrageous than the last. Online, Abigail's image was twisted into ridicule, her name smeared across doctored photos and hateful comments. Hannah felt the dread settle over her like a suffocating fog. This was no longer a game—it was ritual, a collective descent into something darker.

The breaking point came near the school's abandoned gymnasium. The air reeked of damp concrete, the setting as desolate as the act. Olivia, drunk on bravado and cruelty, cornered Abigail. Emily and Emma flanked her, their faces taut with a mixture of fear and excitement. Hannah stood apart, her heart slamming against her ribs, her throat locked in a silent scream. Abigail's terror-stricken eyes mirrored the dread twisting Hannah's gut.

Olivia's words were venom, each insult sharper than the last. Then came the shove. Abigail hit the ground hard, her backpack spilling across the concrete—dog-eared books, scattered pencils, a half-finished drawing of a moonlit forest. As she scrambled to collect them, Olivia's laughter rang out, brittle and triumphant. Emily and Emma joined in, their voices fusing into a cruel chorus.

And then came the kicks. Emily surprised Hannah with her ferocity, her sneaker slamming into Abigail's side. Emma followed, her hesitation evident, but her foot still landing. Olivia was the worst—every blow calculated, every strike punctuated with a shout. Abigail curled into herself, arms shielding her head, her small frame trembling. The sounds of the assault filled the space: the dull thuds of impact, the grunts of exertion, Abigail's muffled pleas.

Hannah stood frozen. Every instinct screamed for her to act, but fear held her captive. She was a prisoner of her own inaction, a silent accomplice to a crime unraveling before her eyes. And in that abandoned gymnasium, beneath the weight of cruelty and silence, something irreversible took root. The memory of Abigail's wide, terrified eyes would haunt Hannah forever—a ghost that refused to fade.

Hannah's mind raced, clawing for an escape route, a reason, anything to break the paralysis that held her captive. A glint of metal caught her eye—a discarded pipe lying nearby. The thought was fleeting and desperate: could she use it to defend Abigail? Or worse… to join in? The terror of that possibility made her recoil inside. She squeezed her eyes shut, unwilling to witness the full extent of their barbarity. When she opened them again, Abigail was still there—a huddled, broken figure on the floor, her breathing ragged, her body already a landscape of bruises.

The raw reality of what they had done—what she had allowed—crashed over Hannah in a suffocating wave. The innocence of the school grounds, the very air they breathed, felt poisoned by violence. The silence that followed was not relief, but soul-crushing shock. The carefree days of middle school had been shattered beyond repair. The weight of it pressed down on Hannah like a shroud, and she knew, with chilling certainty, that nothing would ever be the same. What began as casual cruelty had become something monstrous, and its repercussions would be far darker than any of them could have imagined. Abigail's battered form, left vulnerable in the echoing silence of the gym, was not just a victim—it was a premonition of the path they had chosen.

The aftermath was a blur of adrenaline and fear. The brutal assault left the four girls—Hannah, Olivia, Emily, and Emma—reeling, their young minds struggling to process what they had unleashed. The gymnasium, once just another part of their routine, now radiated menace. Silence hung heavy, broken only by their ragged breaths and the mocking echo of their own laughter. Abigail lay on the concrete, trembling, her bruised face barely recognizable. The ease with which they had inflicted such pain left them shaken, hollow.

Olivia, despite her usual bravado, looked pale, her arrogance stripped away to reveal a flicker of unease. Emily, drained of color, trembled visibly, her aggression curdling into terror. Emma's wide eyes brimmed with disbelief, as if her mind refused to comprehend the scene. And Hannah—her guilt a gnawing, icy weight—felt consumed by despair. The image of Abigail's broken body seared itself into her consciousness, an indictment of her complicity and her silence.

Then, a sound cut through the heavy air: the distant wail of a police siren. Panic hit them like a shockwave. Olivia, her voice hoarse but commanding, snapped, "We need to go. Now. Nobody saw anything. Understand?" Her gaze swept over them, lingering on Hannah—a silent, potent threat. Emily and Emma nodded frantically, terror etched on their faces. Hannah's heart pounded against her ribs; all she could manage was a choked whisper: "Okay."

They scrambled from the gym, their footsteps echoing in the deserted halls. The fragile façade of their friendship was already crumbling under the weight of their secret. Each girl retreated into her own fear, her own guilt, bound together only by silence.

When the police arrived, stern questions and searching gazes forced the girls into performance. Their fabricated story—a tale of accidental bumps and harmless scuffles—tumbled from trembling lips. Their eyes darted, their voices wavered, but they clung to the lie.

Hannah, though, felt the truth pressing on her chest like a stone. Her guilt had already rooted deep, promising a lifetime harvest of nightmares. The silence they clung to was not protection but a prison—a cage of fear and complicity. It would isolate them from the world, from each other, and from themselves. And though their pact bound them together, Hannah knew, with a cold certainty, that the shadow of that day—and the broken girl they left behind—would haunt them forever.

Abigail existed in the quiet corners of Northwood Middle School, a figure easily rendered invisible by the swirling currents of adolescent social life. She was a girl painted in muted watercolors against the vibrant, often garish, backdrop of her peers. Her presence was a whisper, easily lost in the cacophony of slamming lockers and boisterous laughter that defined the school's hallways. Hannah first registered Abigail not through any direct interaction, but through the subtle, almost imperceptible ripple that stirred the air whenever her name was uttered, or more often, when she was pointed out, a silent designation of her outsider status. She was the girl who sought refuge beneath the sprawling branches of the ancient oak tree during lunch, her nose invariably buried in the worn pages of a paperback, a small island of focused serenity in the turbulent sea of teenage drama. Her glasses were perpetually smudged, as if a tangible manifestation of her inability to quite focus on the world around her, and her clothes, chosen with an apparent disregard for fleeting trends, never seemed to quite hang right on her slender frame. She possessed an uncanny ability to fade into the background, a ghost even before she became a memory, her silhouette dissolving into the beige walls of the school.

The initial onslaught of cruelty was almost an art form—small, deliberate cuts designed to chip away at Abigail's already fragile composure. It began at the periphery: whispered comments, pitched just loud enough to be overheard, each word a shard of glass aimed at her spirit. There were the pointed exclusions, the feigned ignorance when she tried to join a conversation, the way her presence was met with averted eyes and stifled giggles.

Hannah remembered one particularly bleak Tuesday, the air heavy with the earthy scent of rain-soaked leaves, when Olivia, with an exaggerated stumble, "accidentally" collided with Abigail in the hallway. The impact sent Abigail's meticulously organized notebooks skittering across the linoleum, pages filled with neat, precise handwriting fanning into chaos. Abigail dropped to her knees, cheeks burning crimson, fumbling to gather her belongings with trembling hands. Olivia offered a saccharine apology, her eyes glittering with amusement—an amusement chillingly devoid of remorse.

A few feet away, Hannah stood frozen, bound by the silent pact with Emily and Emma. The familiar knot tightened in her stomach. She managed only a weak, apologetic smile—a meager acknowledgment of injustice—while her feet refused to move. The unspoken rule of their group demanded silence, demanded complicity. To intervene was to risk exile, to invite the same cruelty upon herself.

But the torment did not stop at whispers or staged collisions. It grew bolder, more insidious, embedding itself into the fabric of Abigail's school life. Her locker combination was altered, a calculated cruelty that left her publicly humiliated as she tugged futilely at the lock, her pleas for help met with a wall of indifferent stares. Soon, anonymous messages appeared on her social media—venomous declarations of her supposed worthlessness, each post a digital echo of her otherness.

Hannah saw them. Sometimes, as she scrolled, her finger hovered over the delete button, torn between conscience and fear. She knew—chillingly, certainly—that these words came from within their circle. Yet terror of ostracization, the primal dread of becoming the next target, held her captive. Olivia's casual dismissal—*"She's asking for it, isn't she?"*—looped in Hannah's mind, each echo twisting the knot in her stomach tighter, a painful reminder of her own cowardice.

The motivations behind their escalating cruelty were a tangled mess of adolescent insecurity and a desperate, often unconscious, hunger for dominance. Olivia, the undeniable ringleader, craved the intoxicating power of control—the validation of dictating the terms of engagement, of deciding who mattered and who did not. Emily, ever the eager acolyte, masked her own insecurities beneath unwavering loyalty, her self-worth tethered to her proximity to Olivia's authority. Emma, quieter but keenly observant, was swept along by the group's momentum, her natural hesitancy repeatedly smothered by the collective force of their will. And Hannah, caught in the undertow, felt the gnawing shame of her passive participation—the agonizing realization that her carefully cultivated politeness was nothing more than a fragile shield for her deeply ingrained cowardice.

They needed a scapegoat, a vessel to absorb the unspoken anxieties, frustrations, and insecurities of their adolescence. Abigail, with her quiet demeanor, gentle spirit, and visible vulnerability, was the perfect target. The thrill of a collective enemy—of a shared purpose, however twisted—carried a magnetic, almost hypnotic pull, dragging them deeper into a vortex of cruelty. Each transgression pushed them further from the shores of decency.

Hannah's politeness, once her armor, began to fray. The cruelties, once subtle and deniable, grew bolder, louder, less concerned with being seen. Whispers in the hallway, once furtive, became open jeers, sharpened and amplified for maximum sting. Abigail's quiet sanctuary under the oak tree was breached with volleys of laughter and hurled insults, shattering the fragile space she had carved for herself.

Hannah was torn in a constant, excruciating battle—between the visceral discomfort twisting in her stomach and the suffocating pressure to remain loyal, to preserve her place within the group. One lunch period remained etched in her memory: Olivia, Emily, and Emma clustered at their usual table, the air thick with the scent of spilled milk and lukewarm pizza. Abigail passed by, her shoulders hunched, her faded backpack slipping precariously. Olivia sighed dramatically, nudging Hannah with a sharp elbow.

"Go on," she hissed, voice laced with challenge. "Tell her that dress makes her look like a potato sack."

Hannah's breath caught in her throat. Her gaze flicked to Abigail's retreating figure—already folding into the anonymity of the crowd—then back to Olivia's unyielding stare. The words lodged in her throat, bitter and immovable. She shook her head, barely perceptible, a silent refusal. Olivia's grin widened, a predator savoring triumph. "Fine," she declared, rising to her feet. Her voice cut through the lunchroom clamor with cruel clarity: "I'll do it myself."

The shame hollowed Hannah out, a suffocating weight pressing on her chest. It was no longer just about Abigail—the quiet girl they were dismantling piece by piece. It was about Hannah's complicity, her paralysis, her betrayal of basic decency. What had started as subtle exclusion had transformed into something calculated and relentless: a systematic erosion of Abigail's very sense of self.

Rumors spread like contagion, insidious whispers infecting the school, targeting Abigail's family, her habits, her supposed eccentricities. Each fabrication was more vicious than the last. Online, under the protection of anonymity, their cruelty flourished unchecked. Snide comments and doctored photos mocked her appearance, extending the torment into every corner of her life. Hannah saw it all—the posts, the laughter behind screens—and a creeping dread settled over her. This was no longer a petty game. It was ritual. It was a descent into something profoundly dark and dangerous—a descent from which she feared there might be no return.

The social sabotage was relentless, a calculated barrage designed to isolate Abigail further. Invitations to parties, weekend hangouts, even casual study groups were "accidentally" withheld, each omission a deliberate act of erasure. Group projects, a staple of school life, came with the unspoken understanding that Abigail would shoulder the bulk of the work—only for her efforts to be dismissed, ignored, or stolen.

Hannah watched as Abigail's isolation deepened. Her quietness hardened into wariness, her once-gentle curiosity replaced by eyes shadowed with constant vigilance. It was a horrifying spectacle, a slow-motion disaster, and Hannah felt trapped—an unwilling spectator in a play she had never consciously agreed to join. Each act of cruelty by her friends mirrored her own receding moral compass, every transgression pulling them further into an abyss Hannah was only beginning to comprehend.

The tipping point came near the school's long-abandoned gymnasium. The air hung heavy with damp concrete and neglect—a fittingly desolate stage for what was about to unfold. Olivia, flushed with bravado and desperate to assert her dominance, had cornered Abigail. Emily and Emma, their faces taut with nervous excitement and uneasy anticipation, flanked her in silent endorsement. Hannah stood apart, her heart pounding like a trapped bird, a scream lodged somewhere between her teeth and her throat. She saw it in Abigail's eyes—raw, unfiltered terror—that mirrored the dread twisting inside her own gut.

Olivia's words were venomous, each insult carefully sharpened to wound. She mocked Abigail's clothes, her intelligence, her very existence. Then, with a brutal shove devoid of pretense, she sent Abigail sprawling across the rough floor. Emily and Emma, caught up in the fever of the moment, joined in—kicks landing with sickening thuds, their laughter sharp and discordant.

Frozen, Hannah stood powerless, a horrified witness to the violence. Abigail curled into herself, arms wrapped around her head, choking back desperate pleas that were drowned out by cruel taunts and jeers. The scene dissolved into a blur of flailing limbs, harsh laughter, and the sickening sounds of impact—a descent into barbarity that chilled Hannah to her core.

Inside, Hannah's conflict reached a breaking point. The moral voice in her head screamed at her to intervene, to push them back, to stop this senseless brutality. But fear held her captive—the instinct to obey, the terror of becoming the next target. Her body betrayed her conscience. She remained frozen, a prisoner of her own inaction, a silent accomplice to the unfolding crime.

The tension was suffocating, the kind of stillness that preceded catastrophe. Hannah felt it in her bones: this was no longer petty schoolyard cruelty. It was something darker, something that would alter all of their lives in ways they could not yet fathom. The image of Abigail's eyes—wide, unblinking pools of fear reflecting the harsh fluorescent light—seared itself into Hannah's memory, a phantom that would haunt her forever.

The air inside the gym thickened with dust and decay, the perfect backdrop for innocence shattering into violence. What began with whispers and rumors had culminated in a savage assault. Olivia, feverish with cruelty, was its architect, her friends—Emily, Emma, and Hannah—reduced to accomplices by action or by silence.

The first shove knocked Abigail hard to the concrete. Her worn backpack spilled open, scattering dog-eared books, sharpened pencils, and a half-finished drawing of a moonlit forest across the floor like fallen leaves. She scrambled to collect them, her hands trembling, movements clumsy with fear. Olivia's brittle laughter, sharp as breaking glass, cut through the silence. Emily and Emma followed her lead, their derision a cruel chorus that filled the abandoned space.

Hannah, rooted in place, felt dread crawl through her veins, every instinct screaming at her to flee, yet her body refused to move. She saw Abigail's face twisted in pain and humiliation, her lips trembling as she fought against tears, her small frame shaking with silent sobs.

Then the kicks began. Not random blows, but calculated, targeted strikes—each one carrying the deliberate intent to hurt. Emily, usually the quieter, more reserved of the group, shocked Hannah with her ferocity. Her small sneaker connected with Abigail's side in a dull, sickening thud. Emma, her face tight with confusion, her eyes wide with dawning horror, followed suit. Her hesitation showed in the way she flinched at each impact, but still, her foot landed, adding to the chorus of escalating violence. Olivia, ever the ringleader, delivered the most brutal blows. Her kicks drove into Abigail's torso and legs, each one punctuated by a guttural shout of triumph.

Hannah's breath caught in her throat, a silent gasp of horror. She saw Abigail curl into herself, arms wrapped tightly around her head, her small body trembling uncontrollably—a fragile vessel battered by the storm of their aggression. The sounds of the assault—the grunts of exertion, the ragged intakes of breath, the sickening thuds of impact—mingled with Abigail's muffled whimpers, forming a grotesque symphony of adolescent barbarity.

Hannah's mind raced, clawing for escape, for a reason to break the inertia that held her captive. Then she saw it: the glint of something metallic, a discarded pipe lying nearby, its rusted surface catching the dim light. A desperate, fleeting thought struck her—could she use it to defend Abigail? Or worse, would she join in? The very notion sickened her, a wave of nausea crashing through her as she recoiled from the possibility of her own capacity for violence. She squeezed her eyes shut, unwilling to witness any more, though the images were already burned into her mind too vividly to erase.

When she opened them again, Abigail was still there—a huddled, broken figure on the floor. Her breathing was ragged, her body a bruised landscape of pain. The raw reality of what they had done—what Hannah had allowed—crashed over her in a suffocating wave of guilt. The innocence of the school grounds, the very air they breathed, felt tainted, poisoned by this betrayal of humanity.

The silence that followed was not relief, but soul-crushing shock. The carefree illusions of middle school had been shattered, replaced by a stark, horrifying truth. The weight of it pressed down on Hannah like a suffocating shroud, and she knew, with chilling certainty, that nothing would ever be the same again. What had begun as casual cruelty had escalated into something monstrous, primal, and terrifying. And Hannah suspected, with growing dread, that the repercussions would be far more horrifying than any of them could yet imagine.

Abigail's broken body, left trembling and alone in the echoing silence of the gymnasium, was not just the aftermath of violence. It was a grim premonition of the dark path they had set in motion— a path from which there might be no return.

The immediate aftermath was a chaotic blur of adrenaline, fear, and the sickening realization of what they had done. The brutal assault on Abigail left the four girls—Hannah, Olivia, Emily, and Emma—reeling, their young minds struggling to process the horror they had just unleashed.

The gymnasium, once a familiar if neglected space, now felt charged with a sinister, oppressive energy. Silence pressed in, broken only by their ragged breaths and the mocking echo of their own laughter—a sound that now seemed alien and chilling. Abigail lay crumpled on the cold concrete, her face swollen, her body trembling with shock. The ferocity of the attack, the ease with which they had inflicted such pain, left them shaken to the core, their bravado stripped away and replaced by a gnawing terror.

Olivia, despite her usual front of confidence, looked pale, her arrogance flickering into unease. Emily trembled visibly, her earlier aggression drained into fear. Emma stood wide-eyed, horror etched across her features, as if her mind could not comprehend the enormity of their crime. And Hannah—her guilt a cold, gnawing weight in her stomach—felt swallowed by despair. The image of Abigail's broken body was seared into her mind, a damning reminder of their collective cowardice.

Then a sound split the heavy air—the distant wail of a police siren. Panic struck like a bolt, seizing their already frayed nerves. Olivia, her voice hoarse but sharp with desperation, hissed, "We need to go. Now. Nobody saw anything. Understand?" Her gaze swept across them, lingering on Hannah with a silent threat. Emily and Emma nodded frantically, their faces pale with terror. Hannah, heart hammering erratically against her ribs, could only choke out a whisper: "Okay."

They scrambled from the gym, their footsteps echoing through deserted corridors. The facade of friendship they had carefully maintained for years crumbled under the weight of their shared crime. Each girl was consumed by fear, bound together not by loyalty but by silence—a brittle conspiracy forged in guilt.

The police arrived with stern questions and probing stares, forcing the girls into a shaky performance of innocence. They clung to a fabricated story—an accidental scuffle, a minor fall. But their trembling voices and darting eyes betrayed the lie. Hannah felt the crushing burden of complicity pressing down on her, her guilt sharper than her friends' frantic attempts at composure.

The seed of guilt had already taken root, promising a harvest of nightmares. The silence they clung to—born of fear—was no shield. It would soon become a prison, isolating them from the world, their families, and even from themselves. Their fragile alliance, forged not in love but in self-preservation, was cemented by dread. Every look felt like an accusation, every whispered word a potential betrayal.

The innocence of youth had been shattered, replaced by the grim reality of guilt and the knowledge that they had irreparably altered not only Abigail's life but their own. The school, once a landscape of trivial struggles and fleeting triumphs, was now a haunted place, stained with violence and cowardice. The memory of Abigail's huddled form, her muffled sobs echoing in the gymnasium, would forever stalk Hannah's conscience—a permanent reminder of the unthinkable act they had committed and the terrible price of their silence.

The receding wail of the siren was a phantom limb, a lingering echo that pulsed in Hannah's ears long after the flashing lights vanished down the tree-lined street. The stark, utilitarian walls of the police station, sterile and impersonal, seemed to press in on her, amplifying the hollowness in her chest. Each question, delivered in calm, measured tones that belied their weight, felt like another stone added to the suffocating burden of guilt she carried. Her own voice, when it finally emerged, was a thin, reedy thread, barely audible above the frantic thumping of her heart.

Olivia, perched on the edge of her chair with unnatural stillness, met Hannah's gaze with something unreadable—a flicker of defiance layered over a desperate plea. Emily, knuckles white against the armrests, stammered nervous, fragmented answers, her wide eyes darting as if searching for an escape hatch that didn't exist. Emma remained predictably silent, her withdrawn presence a heavy cloak that offered no comfort. In that sterile room filled with shared complicity, Hannah felt utterly, terrifyingly alone.

The fabricated narrative—a shove, a fall, a minor disagreement spun out of control—felt brittle, transparent, like glass ready to shatter. Each word was ash in Hannah's mouth, every syllable a betrayal of the reality burned into her memory like a fresh wound. She caught Olivia's subtle nods, the tightening of her jaw, reminders that hesitation could unravel everything. Emily's sobs, interspersed with broken apologies, sounded almost genuine but only underscored the depth of their deception. Emma's monosyllabic responses floated into the void, her gaze fixed far beyond Hannah, as though she had dissociated entirely.

Hannah clung to trivial details—the chipped paint on the interrogation table, the buzzing fluorescent lights, the faint scent of stale coffee in the air. These mundane fragments became anchors, distractions from the storm of guilt and fear tearing through her. Yet the officer's steady, unblinking gaze seemed to bore into her, hunting for truth beneath the lies. A tremor rippled through her. For one terrifying second, she longed to confess, to end the suffocating silence. But then Olivia's eyes caught hers—unyielding, commanding: hold. Keep it together. The unspoken order was clear.

It was a paradox too cruel to ignore: the very act that had fractured them was now the only thing binding them. They were united, not by friendship, but by the crime that shackled them in silence. The weight of it pressed into Hannah's bones, an ache that felt impossible to carry. Outwardly she responded with practiced calm, but beneath, a tempest raged.

Leaving the station was like waking from a nightmare into a world that felt no less hostile. The late afternoon sun, usually a comfort, seemed harsh and accusatory, its long shadows mirroring the darkness festering inside her. Olivia walked ahead, her confident stride an obvious façade. Emily stumbled slightly, her pale face betraying exhaustion. Emma trailed in unnerving stillness. And Hannah, caught in the middle, felt trapped within the suffocating pact they had forged. Their easy camaraderie was gone, replaced by brittle silence where every glance carried accusation, every brush of contact sparked fear.

The walk home was torture. Familiar streets looked alien, menacing. Houses, trees, even the air felt poisoned by their secret. In Hannah's mind, the gymnasium replayed in endless loops: Abigail's broken body, her muffled whimpers drowned by cruelty, the finality of the kicks. The harder Hannah tried to push it away, the sharper the images became.

Olivia broke the silence with false brightness. "So, that's that, I guess. Just a bunch of lies, but hopefully they believe us." In the rearview mirror of her parents' car, her eyes met Hannah's—a silent warning wrapped in reassurance. Emily nodded too eagerly, whispering, "Yeah. We're fine. Nothing happened." Hannah stayed silent in the back seat, the car's close air amplifying her isolation. Outside, familiar houses blurred by, each one a relic of a normalcy that now felt irretrievable.

Their alliance, born of fear, was fragile. Hannah knew with sick certainty that their silence was a dangerous game—a tightrope stretched over a void, where one misstep meant collapse. Already, guilt had begun to take root, whispering doubts, spreading shadows over every thought. Abigail's eyes—wide with terror and pain—haunted her, an unrelenting presence that accused without words.

The shock of the attack was fading, replaced by a more corrosive dread: consequence. The police had seemed satisfied, for now, but Hannah knew their relief was temporary. Olivia wore her mask of composure, but Hannah noticed the tremor in her hands, the flicker of panic in her eyes when no one watched. Emily was unraveling, jumping at the faintest sound, her nerves raw. Emma's silence was no longer passive but defensive, a shield against guilt Hannah knew must be clawing at her too.

The silence that bound them was not peace—it was a living weight. Every creak of the car, every rustle of leaves outside, magnified the unspoken accusations pressing on them. Hannah dissected the gymnasium scene in her mind again and again, tormenting herself with her own inaction. Abigail's crumpled form, her faint gasps for breath, were etched too deeply to ever fade.

And Hannah knew: this was not the end, but the beginning. Their pact of silence was only a fragile dam holding back an inevitable flood. The real horror had yet to unfold. Olivia's shared glance outside the station was a silent oath to deception, but Hannah felt paranoia coil in her chest like barbed wire. The innocence of their middle school days was gone, replaced by a darkness none of them were prepared to navigate.

The silence would only grow louder. What seemed like a shield was in truth a cage, and Hannah could already feel the bars closing in. The fear was not just of being caught—it was of who they had become, of the cruelty they had unleashed. Abigail's tear-streaked, bruised face lingered in her mind, an eternal accuser. And Hannah knew, with crushing certainty, that the weight of their secret would consume them all.

Chapter 2:

The Unraveling Truth

The late afternoon sun, which had felt so accusatory on the drive home, had long since surrendered to twilight. Inside Hannah's bedroom, the familiar glow of her bedside lamp did little to dispel the oppressive darkness pressing in from within her. Sleep was an elusive phantom, insubstantial as the shifting shadows on her walls. Every rustle of leaves outside, every distant car horn, seemed amplified into a monstrous harbinger of doom, each sound another stab of guilt.

She tossed and turned, sheets twisting around her like a suffocating shroud. The image of Abigail's face, contorted in pain, replayed relentlessly behind her eyelids, paired with the phantom echo of her own frantic heartbeat. The fabricated story they had told the police felt like a thin, brittle shell threatening to shatter under the unbearable weight of her conscience. Curled into a trembling ball, knees pulled tight against her chest, Hannah felt consumed by a soul-deep exhaustion that even sleep refused to relieve. The pact of silence no longer felt like protection but like betrayal—of Abigail, and of herself.

It was past midnight when Hannah finally crept out of bed, her bare feet silent against the cool wooden floor. The house lay steeped in heavy slumber, the stillness usually comforting but now charged with menace. She padded down the hallway, each step a negotiation with her own fear. Her mother's bedroom door stood slightly ajar, a sliver of soft golden light spilling into the corridor. A ragged sigh escaped Hannah's lips, nearly swallowed by silence.

She hesitated, her hand hovering above the brass doorknob. Waking her mother, shattering the fragile peace of the house, warred with her desperate need to confess—to unburden herself of the monstrous secret crushing her. The weight was becoming unbearable, a physical ache lodged deep in her chest. She couldn't contain it anymore. Guilt had become poison, spreading through her, unraveling her piece by agonizing piece.

Taking a shaky breath, Hannah pushed the door open and slipped inside. Sarah, her mother, slept soundly, her face softened in the lamplight. A wave of tenderness—and a sharper surge of guilt—washed over Hannah. Her mother looked so peaceful, so unaware of the darkness now consuming her daughter. Hannah stood at the bedside, watching, feeling like an intruder in her own home, tainted by an unspeakable cruelty. Abigail's pleading eyes flashed before her, a silent accusation that churned her stomach.

"Mom?" Hannah whispered, her voice raw and trembling, barely disturbing the stillness. She reached out, brushing her mother's arm with tentative fingers. Sarah stirred, murmuring softly, her breathing shifting as she awoke.

"Hannah? What is it, honey? Are you okay?" Sarah's voice was thick with sleep, her eyes blinking into focus.

"I… I can't sleep," Hannah choked out, her throat tight with unshed tears. Concern swept over Sarah's face, her brow furrowing as sleep slipped away. She sat up and flicked on the bedside lamp, flooding the room with warm light.

"What's wrong? Did you have a bad dream?"

Hannah shook her head, words failing her. The dam of composure broke, and sobs tore free—deep, racking sobs that shook her small body. She crumpled to her knees, burying her face in her mother's side, soaking her nightgown with tears.

Sarah pulled her close, alarm sparking behind her worry. "Hannah, darling, what is it? Please, tell me." Her hand stroked Hannah's hair gently, trying to soothe the storm she could feel raging in her daughter.

Through choking sobs, the words tumbled out in broken confession. "We… we hurt someone, Mom. At school. In the gym. We were mean to Abigail. Really mean. And then… she fell. And we… we kept… we kicked her."

Sarah's arms froze, her breath catching. Her eyes widened in shock as she searched her daughter's tear-streaked face, desperate to believe this was a nightmare, a misunderstanding. But the raw agony in Hannah's eyes told her otherwise.

"Abigail? Abigail Miller?" Sarah whispered, her voice thin with horror.

Hannah nodded, sobbing harder, pulling away as if ashamed to be seen. "We thought it was just a game at first. But then she wouldn't get up. And Olivia said we had to stick together. That no one could know."

Sarah sat in stunned silence, her mind spinning. Abigail—the quiet girl she'd seen before, the one who never quite fit in. And Hannah—her Hannah—confessing to something unthinkable. Shock, grief, and fear battled inside her, but one primal instinct rose above all others: protect her child.

She pulled Hannah close again, whispering, "Oh, Hannah…" Her voice carried sadness, fear, and a desperate attempt to stay composed. "You were brave to tell me."

But then her tone shifted, her fear hardening into urgency. "You said you ran. And you lied to the police. Hannah, you can't tell anyone else about this. Not Olivia, not Emily, not Emma. No one. Do you understand? This has to stay between us. If the truth comes out… you could go to jail."

Hannah's wide eyes brimmed with betrayal. "But, Mom… It's wrong. We hurt Abigail. We should tell the truth."

Sarah cupped her daughter's face, fear sharpening her features. "The truth will only destroy you. You're a child who made a terrible mistake. What matters now is protecting yourself. We have to stay quiet. Pretend it never happened."

Her words, meant as protection, landed like a death sentence. Hannah felt her fragile hope crushed, her mother's reassurance transformed into a cage. The silence that once bound her to her friends now separated her from her mother as well.

And somewhere across town, Abigail's mother, Lauren, drifted through her empty home like a ghost. Each step echoed against the absence of her daughter's laughter. Every photo, every object, was a cruel reminder. Sleep had abandoned her, leaving only a gnawing ache in its place. The world outside spun indifferently on, mocking her grief with its normalcy.

For days, Lauren drifted in a haze of shock—a numb disbelief that offered only a thin, fragile buffer against the onslaught of grief. But numbness, she soon learned, was temporary. Beneath it, a molten rage churned, a furious tide threatening to consume her. It was primal, visceral anger, born from a profound sense of injustice, from the soul-crushing unfairness of it all. Abigail—her bright, beautiful, vibrant Abigail—had been stolen. Not by illness, not by accident, but by the cruel, senseless actions of others. The thought seared her consciousness like a brand, pulsing with every beat of her heart.

The police reports, clinical and detached, reduced Abigail's final moments to sterile jargon—an "incident," a "fall," a "medical emergency." A narrative scrubbed clean of life, of personality, of her daughter's very essence. Yet Lauren sensed a darker truth beneath the surface, one that the authorities seemed determined to bury. She caught it in the subtle evasions, the hushed tones, the way their eyes skittered away when pressed for details. In those silences, in the unsaid, Lauren found the tendrils of suspicion. They knew more. They were protecting someone.

Her world lay fractured, its pieces scattered like shards of glass. The image of Abigail—so full of life just days before—clashed brutally with the chilling permanence of her absence. This was not how it was supposed to be. Abigail was meant to grow, to explore, to stumble and learn, but always to rise again. To be extinguished so carelessly, so brutally, was unforgivable. The injustice festered, a wound refusing to heal, and from that wound, something dark bloomed: a desperate need for answers, a burning hunger for reckoning.

One evening, staring at a framed photograph of Abigail's mischievous smile, the dam finally broke. The fragile wall of denial gave way to a tidal wave of raw fury. Lauren slammed her fist into the wall, the jarring pain a welcome distraction from the deeper ache of her soul. Hot tears streamed down her face—not of sorrow, but of incandescent rage. She wanted to scream, to destroy every object in the house, to unleash the tempest inside her.

"They hurt you," she whispered, guttural and raw. "They took you from me. And they think they can just… get away with it?" The audacity of it, the sheer cruelty, sent a fresh surge of adrenaline through her. Her grief was no longer passive sorrow—it was a weapon, being forged in fire. She would not let Abigail's memory be buried in silence or indifference.

Drawn to Abigail's room, she stepped into the sanctuary frozen in time. Her daughter's perfume still lingered, bittersweet and haunting. Lauren traced the drawings pinned to the corkboard, each one a testament to a vibrant imagination now stilled forever. Then her eyes fell on Abigail's diary, a worn leather-bound book resting on the bedside table. Her hands trembled as she picked it up. Privacy no longer mattered. She needed to know.

The pages overflowed with the earnest scribbles of a teenage girl—crushes, gossip, fleeting worries. But deeper in, the tone darkened. Notes of cruel taunts, whispered threats, and rising fear emerged between the lines. Names appeared—names absent from police accounts, names whispered with urgency that hinted at more than petty schoolyard cruelty. Fear, humiliation, dread bled from the ink.

One entry, scrawled in a shaky hand, chilled Lauren to the bone: *"They cornered me again today. It's getting worse. I'm scared. They said no one will believe me if I tell. That they'll ruin everything. I just want it to stop."* The words confirmed her worst fears. Abigail hadn't simply fallen. She had been hunted. She had been tormented.

Lauren's grief ignited into a terrible purpose. The system had failed. The police had failed. If justice was to be found, she would have to carve the path herself. The thought of Abigail's tormentors walking free while her daughter lay silenced was unbearable.

Her obsession began in the shadows of the internet. She scoured forums, obscure articles, and half-hidden corners where whispers of forgotten lore lingered. She found talk of ancient practices—rituals to reveal hidden truths, incantations to expose secrets, methods of transforming grief and rage into power. A dangerous descent, yes—but fear no longer had a place in her. Rage had eclipsed it.

Soon her study transformed. Once a sanctuary of books and quiet contemplation, it became a crucible of obsession. Abigail's room was too painful—every toy, every book, a stab of loss. Here instead, Lauren surrounded herself with brittle pages and forbidden texts acquired from hushed marketplaces and dim antiquarian shops. The *Necronomicon Excerpts*. *The Book of Shadows – Unveiled*. *Summoning the Unseen: A Practical Grimoire*. Each title was an invocation, a pact, a step further into darkness.

Her fingers, once steady, now moved feverishly across the brittle pages. Letters blurred into sigils, archaic language twisted into cryptic codes she was slowly learning to decipher. Rational thought recoiled—but primal instinct urged her forward. She wasn't merely a mother mourning her child anymore. She was a force of nature, a vessel of maternal fury, prepared to walk through fire. Until those who silenced Abigail were named and broken, Lauren's grief would remain an ember waiting to erupt into a consuming inferno.

She sought not solace, but power. Not understanding, but influence. The official reports were useless; the police interviews, a cruel mockery of justice. They saw a tragedy—an unfortunate accident. Lauren saw a void, a gaping wound ripped open by malice—and she meant to fill it not with tears but with retribution. The idea of communing with Abigail, of speaking to her lost daughter, began as a desperate, fragile hope, a ghost of comfort in the darkness. But as she sifted through incantations and invocations, that desire hardened into something more potent, more demanding. It wasn't only about hearing Abigail's voice; it was about learning who had silenced it—and ensuring they never silenced another.

The air in the study grew heavy, charged with an unseen energy. The usual night sounds—the distant drone of traffic, the chirp of crickets—seemed to recede, held at bay by an invisible barrier. Lauren's breath hitched as she read aloud from a particularly unsettling text, a lament woven into a ritual meant to pierce the veil. The words felt alien on her tongue, thick with an ancient power that vibrated in her bones. Dizziness swept her—intoxicating, disorienting—leaving her both anchored and adrift. The mundane world outside her window, with its predictable cycle of day and night, felt impossibly distant, a realm that no longer held sway.

"Abigail," she whispered—the name a desperate plea that echoed through the unnaturally still room. "My darling Abigail. Can you hear me?" The silence that answered was not empty but pregnant, brimming with an unseen presence—a held breath before a storm. Lauren's skin prickled; sweat beaded at her hairline. The atmosphere shifted, the fabric of reality thinning. Shadows deepened in the corners, coalescing into shapes that flickered at the edge of sight.

She traced a complex diagram from the grimoire—a circle of protection adorned with symbols she didn't fully understand yet instinctively respected. This wasn't only about finding Abigail; it was about surviving the encounter—about not becoming another lost soul in the spectral current she was stirring. The texts warned of dangers: entities that answered such calls, the prices they demanded. Lauren brushed aside the cautions with chilling detachment. What price could be higher than the one she had already paid? What loss greater than the one that had hollowed her out?

Her focus sharpened on a section detailing astral projection and mediumistic communication: attuning to the psychic resonance of the departed, opening channels the living world had closed. Meditation. Visualization. Specific artifacts and chanted phrases. Lauren laid out the items she had gathered: a smooth, dark river stone unnaturally cold to the touch; a sprig of dried rosemary; a silver locket holding a lock of Abigail's hair; and a single unlit black candle.

As she began the incantation, the words felt like a key turning in a lock deep within her. Guttural, resonant, intent-laden, they seemed to bend the air. The room swam; her vision blurred. She closed her eyes and fixed on Abigail: the warmth of her hand, the sound of her laughter, the vibrant life so brutally extinguished. Grief, rage, and desperate yearning fused into a single, blinding point of focus.

Then—a change. The silence broke not with sound but with sensation. A presence. Faint at first, like a breath of cold air on her skin, the fleeting impression of being watched. Her heart pounded. She forced herself to breathe, to follow the instructions. This was the threshold.

She opened her eyes. The unlit candle's wick pulsed with a faint, ethereal blue glow—weak but there. A sign. "Abigail?" she whispered, voice trembling.

A whisper answered—so soft it could have been wind in the leaves or the house settling. But Lauren knew, with a certainty beyond reason, it was Abigail. Her daughter, reaching from the other side. Indistinct, laced with sorrow and confusion: the sound of a soul adrift.

The force she was tapping was raw, untamed, terrifyingly real—like standing at a precipice with the wind clawing her toward the drop. The texts had described the other side not as peace, but as a realm of restless energy, echoes, and fragments of lives. To speak to it was to invite it in, to become a conduit. The cost could be immense—frayed sanity, unwanted attention, vulnerability to malign things.

Cold awareness washed over Lauren: in seeking vengeance, she was opening herself to new dangers. Entities in the liminal dark fed on sorrow and rage—the very essence she was prepared to spend. A faint chuckle rippled at the edge of hearing—not Abigail's, but something ancient and hungry.

She gripped the river stone, the cold anchoring her. Power coursed through—exhilarating, terrifying. No longer merely a grieving mother, she felt like an alchemist of souls, a necromancer-in-training, her desperation her weapon.

The whispers clarified—fragments of feeling more than words: **fear, pain, betrayal**. Not what Abigail would have spoken in life, but the raw residue of her final moments, distorted by the veil. Terror. Confusion. The last desperate struggle. With it came Lauren's rekindled rage, white-hot, stripping away doubt.

She needed more—specifics, faces, voices. The grimoires promised advanced rites to not just connect but reveal: invoking intermediaries, or pouring one's life-force into a beacon to draw the guilty dead. Horrifying—and compelling. If she could see them, name them, she could aim her fury with precision.

The candle's blue light began to pulse in time with her heart. A subtle tug drew at her—something reaching for her through the veil. She held fast, clutching the locket, mind a fortress of grief and resolve. The unraveling now was not only of the mystery of Abigail's death, but of Lauren herself—descending into a world where the living and the dead were divided by a membrane thin enough for a mother's love, and a killer's thirst for vengeance, to pierce. The whispers grew to a roar, and Lauren was ready to answer.

The air crackled—malevolence almost tangible. Eyes sunken, rimmed by sleepless shadows, Lauren traced the final lines of the summoning circle. Not chalk or salt, but a viscous, ink-dark substance with a faint inner shimmer—crushed obsidian, and, she feared with a bone-deep shudder, dried blood.

Grimoires lay open, dog-eared and stained: testaments to sleepless, soul-bartering nights. She was no longer a scholar of the arcane but its instrument.

The rite demanded absolute focus—devotion bordering on self-annihilation. The texts were explicit: to draw a soul from the ether required an offering—not blood or life, but essence, a fragment of the summoner's tether to reality. Lauren had prepared. She shed the layers of her former self—the loving mother, the rational woman, the creature of daylight—and embraced the raw core: grief distilled into an unquenchable thirst for vengeance. This was the price: the immolation of peace and sanity for a chance to reclaim what had been stolen.

With a trembling hand, she lit the final black candle. Its flame was not warm gold but sickly, phosphorescent green. Shadows stretched and twisted, familiar shapes turning grotesque. Rosemary, brittle and desiccated, lay at the cardinal points—its protective virtue warped by the energies she channeled. The river stone pulsed with that same sickly light. In the center, on a velvet cloth, lay the locket—silver tarnished, the lock of hair within seeming faintly luminous.

The chant began—no whisper now, but a low, guttural resonance that shook her ribs. The archaic words, heavy and hot, hammered the veil. A burning chill spread from her core. The air thickened, as if squeezed by an unseen hand. Shadows rose from the floor, swirling like a living shroud.

"Abigail," she crooned, voice raw with tears and effort. "My sweet Abigail. Hear your mother's call. Come home. Come back to me. I have brought you a way." The words were lament, prayer, and demand. She closed her eyes and saw her child as she had been—laughter in the sunlit garden, a small hand in hers, incandescent joy. She poured love, longing, and fury into the vision.

The room pulsed. The house shuddered; panes rattled. Green flames flared, then guttered to pinpricks, as if the very air had been siphoned. Pain lanced her skull—blinding, rending—followed by the nauseous lurch of falling through dimensions.

And then, it began.

A whisper—no longer a diffuse echo, but a nascent presence. Abigail's voice, twisted by the abyss—laced with icy venom and a fury both alien and familiar. Lauren's eyes snapped open.

At the circle's center, a shape coalesced—at first a shimmering distortion like heat haze, then a figure, human and yet unnaturally intense. Abigail—yet not.

The first detail struck like a blow: her hair. Once soft brown, it now cascaded in a torrent of midnight, veined with the candle's sickly green light. It writhed, crackling with unseen energy—no longer merely hair but a living corona of rage.

Her eyes—once innocent—burned as twin embers, points of malevolent green that fixed on Lauren. No recognition. No warmth. Only cold, consuming fury. Spectral lips curved into a predator's smile.

"Mother," the voice hissed—Abigail's, amplified and ancient, forged in rage. The sound of a soul brutalized and remade.

Fear surged—animal, absolute—urging Lauren to flee, to undo what she had wrought. But vengeance overrode it. This was Abigail, yes, but also a weapon.

The revenant lunged with predatory grace. Hair lashed, each strand a whip of energy. An icy gust swept the room, carrying the scent of decay and iron—old blood.

"They hurt me," the specter whispered, the words scraping her nerves. The green embers narrowed, focusing beyond Lauren—as if seeing her tormentors. "They were so cruel. But I remember. I remember everything."

Lauren's heart hammered. She had done it. She had brought her daughter back—but as a revenant, a force born of pain and fury. Power radiated from the figure, a pressure that pinned Lauren in place.

The hair was the crown and the signal—no longer human, but a manifestation of rage, pulsing with inner fire, strands reaching with almost sentient purpose. The unholy magic radiating from it was as exhilarating as it was terrifying.

"Who, Abigail?" Lauren rasped. "Who did this to you?"

The specter tilted her head; the dark, luminous hair flowed like a living cloak. A low, inhuman growl rose. "They will know," she whispered—a promise. "They will all know my wrath. And you, Mother…" The burning gaze returned to Lauren, a flicker—recognition or predatory curiosity— crossing her features. "You helped me. You gave me back my voice. You gave me back my strength."

The green in her eyes brightened, washing Lauren's face in unholy light. A tether cinched tight— psychic, intimate, plunging past flesh into soul. Lauren understood: she hadn't merely summoned a spirit; she had forged a pact with a vengeful entity wearing her daughter's face. Not reunion— collaboration.

The ritual had succeeded, but the cost was far greater than she'd imagined. She had brought Abigail back—and unleashed something ancient and terrible. The revenant stood before her, hair a vortex of vengeful energy—no longer victim but force of nature, embodiment of a mother's rage and a child's eternal suffering. The air thrummed with the dark power Lauren had dared to invoke. This was not the end of grief; it was the beginning of Abigail's revenge—cold, precise, relentless. The pact was sealed. The truth's horror began to reveal itself. Lauren knew she had stepped onto a path with no return—a road paved in shadows and lit by the fire of vengeance. The transformation was complete. The world would learn what a mother's love becomes when twisted by loss and fed by the darkest arts.

The study's oppressive atmosphere—ozone and something acrid, metallic—clung to her skin. The air was too cold, sinking into her bones, an echo of what she had summoned. Abigail—or the terrible semblance of her—had spoken, her promise of retribution hanging in the silence. But the summoning was only a beginning. Lauren knew, with a certainty that gnawed at her, that the energies she'd unleashed would not stay within four walls. They would bleed outward—subtle at first, then undeniable, terrifyingly real.

Across town, in the seemingly mundane hallways of Northwood High, Hannah shivered and pulled her worn denim jacket tighter. It wasn't just the usual early-autumn chill that settled in the building during late afternoons; this was a different kind of cold—creeping, invasive—one that had started a few days after Lauren's desperate plea to the void. It seemed to emanate from nowhere and everywhere at once, raising goosebumps along her arms and prickling the hairs at her nape. She'd mentioned it to Chloe and Maya at lunch, describing it like a freezer door left ajar. Chloe, ever the pragmatist, blamed faulty insulation. Maya, though, had looked at her with wide, perceptive eyes, unease flickering across her face. "It's not just the building, Hannah," she'd whispered. "It feels… wrong. Like something's watching."

That sensation of being watched only intensified. It pricked at the edges of Hannah's awareness, a phantom gaze tracing her movements. Ordinary places turned uncanny: fluorescent lights flickered in the library as she tried to write a history essay; a draft slid through supposedly sealed cafeteria windows; the wind outside would whip into sudden gusts, rattling the glass with a violence out of proportion to the weather.

The unease wasn't Hannah's alone. Chloe arrived one morning paler than usual, dark circles carving hollows beneath her eyes. "I barely slept," she rasped. "The same dream, over and over. I was in a dark place, and something was hunting me. There was whispering, but not words I understood—just a low, menacing murmur." Maya nodded, grim. "I had a similar dream. Only in mine, the whispers were clearer. They were calling my name. Not friendly. Hungry."

The collective dread began to fray their nerves. The school—once a familiar backdrop—felt like a character in a horror film. Lockers loomed larger, metallic faces reflecting sterile light like gaping maws. Shadows pooled deeper in classroom corners, gathering as if to solidify. Even the scent of floor wax and teenage sweat was overlaid by something dank and cold, like the breath of a tomb.

One afternoon, as the three walked to the bus stop, the cloud-dappled blue sky abruptly darkened. A thick, unnatural fog rolled in from the woods at the town's edge, a disorienting gray shroud that swallowed the landscape. It clung low, damp and cloying, and within minutes, visibility dropped to a few feet. The temperature plunged; the earlier chill sharpened into a bite that stole their breath.

"This is weird," Chloe muttered through chattering teeth. "The forecast said clear skies all week."

"It's like the world is holding its breath," Maya said, eyes darting into the swirl. "Or reacting to something."

Hannah's heart began to thrum. She couldn't shake the sense that this sudden shift was tied to the subtle wrongness creeping into their days—as if reality itself were fraying and they were caught in the widening tear. Laughter from other students, usually comforting, sounded brittle and hollow, easily swallowed by the fog's oppressive hush. The distant groan of trees took on a mournful edge, as though the natural world sensed the intrusion of something profoundly unnatural and recoiled. The air felt heavy, charged with unseen energy that made Hannah's skin crawl—pressing in, a silent testament to forces newly at play. The path to the bus stop, usually a casual stroll, became an alien corridor of gray, each step a venture into the unknown. The fog seemed to whisper—a low, sibilant brush at their ears—carrying damp-earth scent and a faint metallic tang, like old pennies left in the rain.

Huddled against the cold and their growing fear, Hannah thought of her aunt Lauren—eccentric, fond of late nights and old books, lately distant and shadowed by grief. An image flashed, unbidden: Lauren's study, crowded with strange artifacts and an unsettling quiet. Then another—clearer—of Lauren's hands, stained with something dark, tracing intricate patterns on a floor. A shiver—unrelated to the temperature—ran down Hannah's spine. The fog thickened, muffling the world, isolating them. Even their friendship felt fragile, threatened by a pervasive wrongness unspooling their lives. The only sound was her own heartbeat, a frantic drum against the unnatural stillness. The prickling at her neck sharpened into certainty: they were no longer alone. The whispers rose—a chorus now, indistinct voices coiling around them.

Maya gasped, pointing toward the fog's edge. "Did you see that?" she breathed. "Something moved."

Hannah squinted into the gray. For a heartbeat, she saw it too—a patch darker than the rest, a shape that writhed with an unnatural fluidity, not branches swaying. Then it was gone, swallowed by the veil.

"Probably just a shadow," Chloe said, but without conviction. "Or a deer. Or… something."

Hannah knew it was neither. The air crackled with tension that tightened her chest. The whispers, briefly receded, surged back—louder, insistent—swirling like unseen specters. Still indecipherable, but their intent felt clear: a predatory hunger reaching out from the fog. The bus stop—a beacon of routine moments before—now seemed an exposed precipice, a lonely outpost at the edge of something vast and terrifying. The world felt distorted, as if the natural order had been deliberately subverted. Shadows in the mist stretched and warped, hinting at shapes that defied reason. The sense of being watched became a suffocating weight, a presence pressing from all sides. Even the air tasted metallic and cold, threaded with the faint odor of decay.

"We need to get out of here," Hannah said, voice tight. "Now."

They turned—and a violent gust tore through the fog, whipping their clothes and scattering dead leaves in spirals. It wasn't mere wind; it felt directed, a blast of ice carrying a low, guttural sigh from the ground itself. The bus-stop sign swayed on its metal pole, its lettering blurred by the churn. Dread spiked—pure, animal urgency. They ran. Their footsteps echoed oddly in the muffled world, fog clinging like a shroud, whispers pursuing as a disembodied chorus through the deepening gloom. The world had tilted, and they were falling into a darkness they could not comprehend—heralded by a chill that promised more than winter.

Then came the worst part: the stillness after. Silence, thick and menacing, seemed to swallow familiar sounds, leaving only the thunder of their heartbeats and the whispers that now felt as though they rose from inside their own minds. The fog became a boundary made skin—tangible dread separating their reality from whatever had intruded. With every passing moment inside its grasp, its hold deepened, drawing them farther into its unnatural cold. The air hummed with latent power, a discordant resonance vibrating in their bones—a premonition of an unraveling truth just beyond the veil of ordinary life. They were no longer simply teenagers walking home from school; they were unwitting participants in a dawning horror. And the first cold tendrils of that horror had already wound around them, promising a descent into a nightmare from which there might be no waking.

Chapter 3:

The First Victim

The chill that had settled over Northwood High seemed to follow Olivia home, seeping through the cracks of her old Victorian house like an unwelcome guest. It wasn't just the drafty windows or the ancient heating system—this was a deeper cold, a marrow-deep chill that no amount of blankets or hot chocolate could drive away. For days she had fought a creeping unease, the sense that her familiar surroundings had grown subtly, terrifyingly alien.

It began with small things: the floorboards creaking when she was certain no one else was home, the faint suggestion of movement just beyond her peripheral vision, the prickling sensation of eyes on her even when she sat alone in her room, bathed in the sterile glow of her laptop.

Her house, once a sanctuary of worn comfort and familiar clutter, now felt like a stage set for a play she hadn't agreed to perform in. The portraits of stern-faced ancestors lining the hallway seemed to follow her with their painted eyes—no longer merely historical, but accusatory. The antique grandfather clock, a silent sentinel for decades, had begun to chime at odd hours, its sonorous notes echoing through the house like a mournful lament. At night, Olivia lay awake in bed, heart hammering, straining to identify the source of every groan of timber, every scrape of branches against glass. She tried to rationalize it, of course.

Her parents were away on a business trip, leaving her alone for the week. Stress, she told herself. The weight of college applications, the fallout with Hannah and Chloe, the lingering unease after the incident at the football game—plenty of reasons to feel on edge.

But the dread persisted, gnawing at her focus until she could no longer concentrate. Textbooks blurred into meaningless symbols, her thoughts consumed by phantom sounds and fleeting shapes. One evening, while forcing herself through a history paper, the sensation struck hard: a distinct prickling at the back of her neck, as if someone were standing directly behind her. She spun around to find only the empty living room, bathed in the glow of a single lamp. The feeling didn't fade—it pressed against her skin, invasive and unrelenting. She doused the lamp, plunging the room into darkness, as if hiding could protect her from the unseen gaze. The silence that followed was suffocating, broken only by the frantic pounding of her heart.

She told herself it was imagination—too much caffeine, not enough sleep. She was the pragmatic one, the sensible one. Hannah was the dreamer, the one who found patterns in shadows. Maya was the intuitive one, attuned to invisible currents. Olivia was meant to be the anchor, the skeptic, the steady voice. But her carefully constructed facade of logic was cracking. Alone, her bravado dissolved, leaving behind something raw, fragile, and exposed.

The feeling of being watched only grew stronger. It wasn't confined to the house anymore—it followed her everywhere. Walking to the corner store, she felt eyes in the alley shadows. In a quiet café, the murmur of strangers' conversations seemed to curl toward her, carrying whispers meant for her ears alone. Even checking her phone became unsettling, the screen's glow charged with a vague, malignant threat. She began avoiding mirrors, recoiling from the strained reflection of her own pale face, eyes wide with unspoken fear.

She remembered Hannah's hushed confession of the chill creeping through Northwood High, Chloe's restless nights, Maya's whispered dreams. At the time, Olivia had dismissed it all, offering rational explanations, even teasing Hannah for her sensitivity. But now those memories returned with chilling weight. What if it wasn't coincidence? What if the strange occurrences were not isolated incidents at all, but threads in a larger, more sinister pattern? The thought cut through her with a fresh wave of icy dread.

One afternoon, desperate for a distraction, Olivia decided to visit the library, hoping the quiet hum of activity and the familiar scent of old paper would offer some solace. She found a secluded carrel at the back, surrounded by towering shelves of forgotten lore. As she tried to focus on a research paper, a cold draft snaked around her ankles, despite the windows being closed and the air conditioning barely on. She shivered, pulling her cardigan tighter. Then, she heard it – a faint, almost imperceptible scratching sound, coming from within the wall beside her. She froze, listening intently. Scratch. Scrape. Pause. Scratch. It sounded like something alive, something desperate to escape.

Her breath hitched. This wasn't just stress. This wasn't an overactive imagination. This was something real, something tangible, and terrifyingly present. She tried to tell herself it was just mice, a common problem in old buildings like the library. But the sound was too deliberate, too rhythmic, too… intelligent. It was as if whatever was making the noise was aware of her, toying with her. She glanced around, her eyes darting from one silent reader to another, but no one else seemed to notice. They were lost in their own worlds, oblivious to the subtle horror unfolding just inches away. The scratching continued, growing bolder, more insistent, vibrating through the wooden table, up her arms, and into her very bones. A prickle of sweat broke out on her forehead. She wanted to scream, to bolt from the library and never look back, but her feet felt rooted to the spot, paralyzed by a fear she couldn't overcome.

Olivia closed her eyes, forcing herself to take slow, deep breaths. She had to be strong. She couldn't let this get to her. She imagined herself back in the gym, hands gripping the handlebars of her bike, muscles burning, focus absolute. That was strength. This fear, this paralyzing dread, was not strength. It was weakness. But the internal battle was exhausting, and the scratching sound seemed to mock her every attempt at resilience.

When she finally forced herself to leave the library, the world outside seemed muted, as if the oppressive atmosphere of the building had followed her. The sky was a bruised, heavy grey, and the air felt thick, stagnant. As she walked, she noticed a shadow detach itself from the side of a building and glide unnervingly across the sidewalk ahead of her, a fleeting, serpentine movement that made her stomach churn. It was too deliberate to be a trick of the light, too fluid to be a person. It was as if the very geometry of the world was subtly distorting, bending to the will of something unseen.

Back in her empty house, the silence was amplified. Every ticking clock, every creak of settling wood seemed to announce her solitude, her utter isolation. She found herself scanning the windows, convinced she saw movement at the periphery, a flicker of something dark and indistinct. She began to question her sanity. Was she truly experiencing these things, or was her mind creating them, a twisted manifestation of her anxieties? The lack of anyone to confide in gnawed at her. Hannah was caught up in her own growing unease, and Maya and Chloe were a unit, often lost in their shared experiences. Olivia felt adrift, her usual social circle offering no comfort when she couldn't even articulate the nature of her fear. What would she even say? "I think I'm being watched by shadows, and the walls are scratching at me"? They'd think she'd finally lost it. The isolation was a breeding ground for her fear, allowing it to fester and grow unchecked. Her bravado, the carefully constructed wall of composure she presented to the world, was slowly crumbling, revealing the terrified girl beneath, a girl who was beginning to realize that the comforting illusions of safety and normalcy were perhaps the most dangerous lies of all. The weight of this unspoken terror was crushing her, pressing down on her chest, making each breath a conscious, labored effort. She was alone, truly alone, in a world that was rapidly becoming indistinguishable from a nightmare, and the terrifying realization was dawning that she might be the first to truly understand how deep the darkness went.

The fluorescent lights of the girls' restroom flickered with a weak, insistent pulse, casting long, distorted shadows across the sterile tile floor. The air hung thick with the cloying scent of cheap floral air freshener, a pathetic attempt to mask the usual undercurrents of disinfectant and something else, something vaguely metallic, that Olivia couldn't quite place. It was late afternoon, the school day winding down, and most students had already fled the building, eager for the freedom of the outside world. Olivia, however, had lingered, driven by a desperate need to wash the lingering grime of anxiety from her hands, to splash cold water on her face, and to try to convince herself that the growing dread was merely a figment of her overtaxed imagination.

She'd chosen this particular restroom, the one on the less-trafficked second floor near the old art wing, precisely because it was usually deserted at this hour. She craved solitude, the illusion of safety in emptiness. But as the heavy metal door clanged shut behind her, a cold wave of unease, far more potent than the ambient chill of the building, washed over her. The silence that descended was not the peaceful quiet she had hoped for, but a heavy, suffocating stillness, as if the very air was holding its breath. The buzzing of the fluorescent tubes overhead seemed to intensify, morphing into a low, guttural hum that vibrated deep within her skull.

Olivia walked toward the row of sinks, her footsteps echoing unnervingly on the tiled floor. She avoided her own reflection in the large, grimy mirror, her gaze fixed instead on the row of chipped porcelain sinks, each stained with the ghosts of countless hurried washes. The lockers lining the opposite wall stood like silent, watchful sentinels, their metal doors reflecting the unsteady light in dull, metallic glints. Every instinct screamed at her to turn and flee, to burst back out into the relative normalcy of the empty hallway, but a morbid curiosity, a desperate need to confront whatever it was that had been haunting her, kept her rooted to the spot.

As she reached for the faucet, her fingers brushing against the cold, damp metal, a faint sound reached her ears. It was a whisper, barely audible above the incessant hum of the lights, yet it seemed to coil around her, icy and sharp. She froze, her hand hovering over the faucet.

"You shouldn't be here."

The voice was thin, reedy, like dry leaves skittering across pavement. It was undeniably feminine, yet stripped of any warmth or humanity. Olivia's heart leapt into her throat, a wild bird trapped in a cage of ribs. She spun around, her eyes scanning the dimly lit space. The stalls were all empty, their doors ajar, revealing nothing but the cold, hard angles of porcelain and metal. The mirrors offered only the distorted, shimmering reflections of the flickering lights.

"Hello?" she called out, her voice trembling, a pathetic squeak in the oppressive silence. "Is someone there?"

There was no response, only the maddening hum of the lights and the frantic thumping of her own pulse. She took a hesitant step toward the nearest stall, her hand outstretched, ready to push open the door. As her fingers made contact with the cool metal, a blast of frigid air, impossibly cold, washed over her, stealing her breath and raising goosebumps on her arms. It felt like standing in the path of an arctic wind, yet there was no visible source, no open window, no draft.

And then she saw her.

Or rather, she glimpsed her. A flicker of movement at the edge of her vision, a distortion in the air near the back wall, beside the overflowing trash can. It was a shape, indistinct and wavering, like heat rising from asphalt, but imbued with a chilling darkness. For a fleeting second, Olivia thought she saw a face, pale and gaunt, with eyes that burned with an ancient, unholy rage. Abigail. The name surfaced unbidden in her mind, a cold, hard stone dropping into the pit of her stomach. It was Abigail, the girl from the football game, the one whose vacant stare had haunted her ever since. But this wasn't the withdrawn, almost spectral Abigail she remembered from the stands. This was something… else. Something predatory.

The figure seemed to coalesce for a moment, a fragile silhouette against the grimy tiles, before dissolving back into the shadows as if it had never been. But the impression remained, burned into Olivia's retinas: the stark white of a school uniform, the unnaturally still posture, the unnerving absence of breath. The whisper returned, closer this time, a venomous hiss that seemed to emanate from everywhere and nowhere at once. "You saw. You know."

A wave of pure, unadulterated terror surged through Olivia, freezing her blood. Her muscles locked, her lungs seized, and for a terrifying moment, she was utterly incapable of movement, of thought, of anything but the overwhelming presence of the entity before her. It felt like a physical weight pressing down on her, suffocating her, its chilling aura seeping into her very core. Her mind, so adept at rationalization and denial, was overwhelmed. There was no logical explanation for this. This was not stress. This was not an overactive imagination. This was real. Terrifyingly, undeniably real.

She could feel its gaze on her, a palpable, icy scrutiny that stripped away every last vestige of her composure. It was a gaze that saw through her carefully constructed defenses, a gaze that knew her deepest fears and found them wanting. The air around her grew colder still, so cold that her teeth began to chatter uncontrollably. She squeezed her eyes shut, a desperate attempt to block out the terrifying apparition, to retreat back into the familiar darkness of her own mind. But the cold, the whispers, the suffocating presence – they were all too real to ignore.

"It's not over," the voice whispered again, its tone laced with a cruel amusement that sent shivers down her spine. "It's just beginning."

Olivia's knees buckled. She stumbled backward, her hand scrabbling for the cold, hard surface of the wall for support. Her breath came in ragged gasps, each inhale a searing pain, each exhale a desperate plea for escape. She could feel it drawing closer, a subtle shift in the atmosphere, a tightening of the suffocating dread. It was as if the very space around her was contracting, squeezing her, holding her captive.

She risked a glance toward the mirrors again. The flickering lights seemed to mock her, their unsteady glow casting grotesque, dancing shadows that writhed and contorted like malevolent specters. And then, in the mirror directly in front of her, she saw it. Not a reflection of Abigail, but a reflection of the space behind her, a distortion in the glass, a rippling darkness that seemed to pulse with an unnatural energy. It was an absence of light, a void that defied the harsh glare of the fluorescent tubes.

A primal scream tore from her throat, a raw, guttural sound of pure terror that echoed through the empty corridor. She didn't wait to see what would happen next. Adrenaline, a potent surge of pure survival instinct, coursed through her veins, overriding the paralysis of fear. She turned and bolted, her legs pumping, her lungs burning, pushing through the heavy metal door and bursting out into the relative safety of the hallway. She didn't dare look back, the chilling whispers and the suffocating cold pursuing her like a tangible entity. She ran, her heart hammering against her ribs like a drumbeat of pure terror, the image of the void in the mirror seared into her mind. The girls' restroom, once a mundane sanctuary of teenage girlhood, had become a terrifying portal, a place where the veil between worlds had thinned, and something ancient and hungry had found her. The encounter, however brief, had irrevocably changed her, shattering the last vestiges of her skepticism and plunging her headlong into the chilling reality of what was to come. She was no longer just a witness; she was a target. And the darkness had finally found her.

The cold hadn't left Olivia. Even now, miles away from the echoing, sterile horror of the girls' restroom, cocooned in the faux security of her bedroom, the chill clung to her like a second skin. The memory of Abigail's vacant stare, of the void in the mirror, was a constant, gnawing presence. Sleep offered no respite; her dreams were a chaotic tapestry of flickering lights, whispered accusations, and the suffocating sensation of being trapped. She was a prisoner in her own mind, haunted by a terror she couldn't rationally explain, yet couldn't deny.

The gnawing unease had been building for days, a subtle shift in the atmosphere of Northwood High, a pervasive sense of dread that seemed to settle over the students like a shroud. Whispers had begun to circulate, hushed and fragmented, of unsettling incidents, of strange occurrences that defied logical explanation. Most dismissed them as locker-room gossip, the usual teenage hyperbole. But Olivia knew. She had seen. She had felt.

The following afternoon, the dread that had been a low thrum in the background escalated into a piercing shriek. It began, as most things did now, with a feeling. A prickling sensation on the back of her neck, the undeniable certainty of being watched. She was in the library, ostensibly studying for a history test, but her focus had fractured days ago. The quiet hush of the library, usually a sanctuary, now felt pregnant with unspoken threats.

She looked up from her textbook, her gaze sweeping across the rows of shelves, the scattered clusters of students hunched over their work. Nothing seemed out of the ordinary. Yet, the feeling persisted, a cold, clammy dread that seeped into her bones. Then, her eyes landed on a figure at the far end of the aisle, partially obscured by a towering bookshelf. It was a girl, dressed in the familiar, drab uniform of Northwood High. Her back was to Olivia, her posture unnervingly still.

It was Abigail.

Olivia's breath hitched. Abigail hadn't been seen at school for weeks, not since the football game, since that night. The whispers had intensified after her disappearance—tales of a breakdown, of being sent away. But here she was, standing as if she had never left. A ripple of unease, colder than any she had felt before, coursed through Olivia. Abigail's presence was a violation of the natural order, a chilling echo from a place she should no longer occupy.

As Olivia watched, mesmerized by a morbid fascination, Abigail slowly turned her head. Her face was pale, almost translucent, her eyes sunken and shadowed, yet burning with an unnerving intensity that seemed to pierce through the distance, directly at Olivia. There was no recognition in those eyes, no flicker of a shared past, only an ancient, consuming emptiness that mirrored the void Olivia had glimpsed in the restroom.

A silent scream clawed at Olivia's throat. She wanted to run, to scramble out of the library and disappear into the crowded hallways, but her feet were rooted to the spot. Abigail's gaze held her captive, a silent, terrible summons. And then, a strand of hair, impossibly dark and thick, detached itself from Abigail's tightly wound bun. It seemed to lengthen, to writhe—a living tendril of darkness that slithered through the air, defying gravity and the ambient stillness of the library.

The hair moved with an unnerving purpose, not like a falling strand, but like a predator sensing its prey. It glided through the air, a serpentine shadow, bypassing desks and students, its trajectory unerringly fixed on Olivia. A collective gasp, a ripple of startled murmurs, spread through the library as others noticed the bizarre spectacle. But before anyone could react, before Olivia could even register the full horror of what was happening, the hair was upon her.

It wrapped around her ankle with an impossible, vice-like grip. Olivia cried out, a strangled gasp of pain and shock, as the coarse strands tightened, biting into her skin. She tried to wrench her foot away, but the hair held fast, unyielding. Another strand snaked out, then another, rising from Abigail's head like an anaconda's coils. They were impossibly strong, impossibly fast, thicker than any natural hair, possessing a chilling sentience.

28

Panic, sharp and absolute, seized Olivia. She stumbled, her hands flailing for purchase, her history textbook tumbling to the floor with a thud that was lost in the rising cacophony of screams. The hair was everywhere now, a suffocating web of darkness. It wrapped around her waist, her arms, her chest, each strand tightening with a relentless, suffocating pressure. It was like being caught in a thousand living ropes, each one imbued with a chilling strength that defied human comprehension.

Olivia thrashed, desperate to break free, to tear herself away from this impossible, horrifying embrace. But it was useless. The hair was an extension of Abigail's will, a manifestation of her distilled rage and pain. It tightened with cold, calculating precision, the strands digging into Olivia's flesh, drawing blood. The coarse texture scraped against her skin, a horrifying, intimate violation. She could feel it constricting her lungs, stealing her breath, the very air around her growing cold and heavy.

"Let go!" she choked out, her voice thin and reedy, lost in the panicked chaos erupting around her. Students were scrambling from their seats, their faces contorted in terror, pointing and shrieking at the grotesque tableau unfolding before them. The librarians, usually figures of calm authority, were frozen, their faces pale masks of disbelief and horror.

Abigail remained at the end of the aisle, her expression unreadable, her eyes fixed on Olivia. There was no malice on her face, no triumph, only a chilling, profound emptiness, as if she were merely an instrument of a force far greater, far more ancient than herself. The hair continued its relentless work, a testament to a power Olivia couldn't begin to comprehend. It was a weapon born of an unspeakable grief, a manifestation of a soul twisted by trauma, now enacting a gruesome, spectral revenge.

Olivia felt a searing pain shoot through her chest as the hair tightened, the strands constricting around her ribs like a medieval torture device. She gasped, her vision blurring, the edges of her world darkening. She could feel her bones beginning to creak under the immense, unnatural pressure. The hair wasn't just restraining her; it was crushing her. The sound of splintering bone, a sickening crack, echoed in the sudden, terrifying silence that had fallen over the library, a silence punctuated only by Olivia's ragged, dying breaths.

Her struggles grew weaker, her body succumbing to the overwhelming force. The hair continued its relentless advance, inching its way toward her face, its dark tendrils caressing her skin with an icy touch. She could feel it creeping into her mouth, her nostrils, the suffocating embrace tightening around her very essence. The last thing Olivia registered was the unnerving stillness of Abigail's gaze, the profound absence of anything human within it, as the world around her dissolved into a suffocating, all-consuming darkness. The hair, Abigail's strangling hair, had claimed its victim, a brutal, horrifying testament to a revenge that transcended life itself. The whispers that had been circulating about Abigail were no longer just whispers. They were a chilling prophecy, a harbinger of a darkness that had finally, and irrevocably, descended upon Northwood High. The terror was no longer a shadow; it was a tangible, murderous force.

The silence that followed Olivia's death was a heavy, suffocating blanket thrown over Northwood High. It wasn't the quiet of respect or solemn contemplation, but the suffocating stillness of profound shock, the kind that precedes a scream or the deafening roar of a tidal wave. The discovery of Olivia's body in the library, amidst scattered textbooks and overturned chairs, had sent a tremor through the otherwise placid surface of the school's routine. It was too public, too bizarre, too… impossible.

When the first responders arrived, the scene was one of utter bewilderment. Olivia, or what was left of her, was a macabre tableau. Her limbs were splayed at unnatural angles, her skin stretched taut over bone, giving her a gaunt, almost skeletal appearance. The constricting marks around her throat and chest were not bruises, but deep, indelible lines, as if she had been squeezed by an unseen, impossibly strong force. There were no signs of struggle in the conventional sense—no torn clothing beyond what the hair had inflicted, no disarray suggesting a physical fight. The only disturbance was the unnatural positioning of her body, like a puppet with its strings violently severed, and the unsettling stillness of her vacant eyes, which seemed to stare accusingly at the ceiling, at a world that had failed to protect her.

Detective Miller, a man whose jaded demeanor usually masked a keen intellect, found himself staring at the body with a growing sense of unease. He had seen death in its myriad forms: the brutal finality of a gunshot, the messy aftermath of a stabbing, the quiet surrender of old age. But this… this was different. The sheer impossibility of it gnawed at him. How could a teenager, healthy and vibrant one moment, be found dead in such a gruesome fashion without any discernible weapon or assailant? The coroner's preliminary findings were even more perplexing. No broken bones, save for a few hairline fractures that suggested immense pressure, and no traces of poison or drugs. The cause of death was listed as asphyxiation, but the mechanism remained a chilling enigma. The sheer force required to inflict such damage, without leaving any physical evidence of the perpetrator, was beyond anything Miller had encountered in his twenty years on the force. It was as if Olivia had been crushed by the very air around her.

The news spread like wildfire, fueled by the hushed, terrified whispers of the students. Olivia, the bright, artistic girl, the one who always had a sketchbook in hand, was gone. And the manner of her death was so horrific, so inexplicable, that it quickly transcended the usual tragedy of a student passing. It became a legend in the making, a dark fairy tale whispered in the halls, each retelling more gruesome, more unbelievable than the last. The library, once a sanctuary of knowledge and quiet study, was now a crime scene, a place of dread, its imposing shelves now seeming to loom like silent, judgmental witnesses.

Hannah and Emma, Olivia's closest friends, were inconsolable. The initial shock had been a numbing disbelief, a refusal to accept the horrifying reality. They had clung to each other, their world collapsing around them. They remembered Olivia's growing fear in the weeks leading up to her death, her fragmented accounts of unsettling occurrences, her hushed worries about Abigail. At first, they had dismissed her anxieties as stress, as the overactive imagination of a teenager dealing with the pressures of high school. But now, faced with the brutal finality of Olivia's demise, their denial shattered, replaced by a chilling, burgeoning suspicion.

They had seen Abigail. Not in the flesh, not at the scene of Olivia's death, but they had seen her. Or rather, they had felt her presence. A week before Olivia's death, during a particularly tense study session in Emma's basement, a palpable chill had descended, far colder than the autumn air outside. The lights had flickered, and a low, guttural whisper had seemed to emanate from the shadows, a sound that was both familiar and utterly alien. Emma had sworn she had seen a fleeting glimpse of Abigail's face in the darkened reflection of a window, her eyes hollow and filled with an ancient sorrow. Hannah, more practical and grounded, had initially tried to rationalize it, blaming faulty wiring or an overactive imagination fueled by too much caffeine and too little sleep. But even she couldn't shake the feeling of dread that had settled over them that night, the unnerving certainty that something was terribly wrong.

Now, sitting in Emma's living room, the news of Olivia's death a fresh wound, the pieces began to click into place with a horrifying, sickening clarity. Abigail, who had vanished after the football game and had been rumored to be struggling with mental health issues, was back. And not in a way anyone could have imagined. The whispers, the strange occurrences, Olivia's increasing fear— it all pointed to something far beyond the realm of ordinary human behavior.

"It was her, wasn't it?" Hannah choked out, her voice thick with unshed tears. Her gaze was fixed on the television, where a reporter was breathlessly recounting the details of the discovery, her voice laced with an almost palpable fear. "Olivia… she was right, wasn't she? About Abigail."

Emma could only nod, her own tears finally spilling over, tracing a path through the dust of the day's events. The image of Abigail, her eyes vacant and unnervingly still during that brief, terrifying encounter in the library, flashed in her mind. It wasn't just the look; it was the aura of cold, desolation that surrounded her, a presence that felt ancient and wrong. Abigail had always been quiet, a little lost, but never like this. Not with that… void.

"But how?" Emma whispered, her voice barely audible. "How could she… do this? It's impossible. It's not real." Yet, even as the words left her lips, the chilling certainty settled in her heart. It was real. The terror they had felt, the strange occurrences, Olivia's death – it was all interconnected, a terrifying chain of events set in motion by something they couldn't yet fully comprehend. Abigail was back, and she was a harbinger of a darkness that had finally descended upon Northwood High.

The grief was a crushing weight, but beneath it, a new emotion began to stir: a cold, creeping fear. The kind of fear that paralyzed, that whispered insidious doubts, that made them question everything they thought they knew. The police were baffled, the community was in an uproar, but Hannah and Emma knew, with a certainty that chilled them to the bone, that this was no ordinary crime. This was something else.

Something ancient. Something hungry. And as they looked at each other, their faces pale and drawn, they knew their nightmare had only just begun. Olivia was the first victim, a brutal testament to a power that had been unleashed. And they, her friends, were left to pick up the pieces, to confront a horror that defied logic, and to face the chilling possibility that they might be next.

The days that followed Olivia's death were a blur of hushed conversations, averted glances, and a pervasive sense of unease that hung over Northwood High like a shroud. The library remained closed, its entrance cordoned off with yellow police tape, a stark, somber reminder of the unfathomable tragedy that had occurred within its hallowed halls. Students walked the corridors with a newfound wariness, their youthful exuberance replaced by a grim, watchful apprehension. Every shadow seemed to hold a lurking threat, every whispered conversation a harbinger of doom.

Detective Miller found himself facing a wall of silence, not just from the students, but from the very nature of the crime itself. The lack of physical evidence was a gaping hole in his investigation, a void that logic couldn't fill. He interviewed teachers, staff, and dozens of students, meticulously piecing together Olivia's last known hours. But no one had seen anything definitive. A few recalled Olivia looking distressed, her eyes darting nervously around the library, but that was it. The supernatural elements, the whispers about Abigail, were dismissed by most as the usual gossip and hysteria that followed a tragic event. Yet, the lack of any conventional explanation gnawed at Miller. He was a man of facts, of evidence, of tangible proof. But Olivia's death offered none of that. It was as if she had simply… dissolved.

Hannah and Emma, meanwhile, were living in a constant state of heightened anxiety. The grief over Olivia's loss was compounded by a terrifying understanding of its cause. They avoided the library, their once-familiar sanctuary now a place of pure dread. Every time the school lights flickered or a gust of wind rattled the windows, their hearts leaped into their throats. They confided in each other, their hushed conversations filled with fragmented memories of Abigail, of Olivia's increasing paranoia, of the unsettling events that had preceded the tragedy.

"It's not just in our heads, Em," Hannah insisted, her voice a low, urgent whisper as they sat in Emma's bedroom, the curtains drawn tightly against the encroaching twilight. "We felt it. We saw her. Olivia saw her too. Abigail is back, and she's… she's not Abigail anymore."

Emma nodded, her own fear a cold knot in her stomach. The memory of Olivia's last, terrified message, a garbled voicemail filled with desperate pleas and the sound of something scraping against a hard surface, played on repeat in her mind. Olivia had tried to warn them, but in their youthful ignorance, they had failed to truly listen.

Now, the weight of that failure was crushing.

"What do we do, Hannah?" Emma's voice trembled. "The police don't believe us. They think we're just kids making up stories."

"We have to figure this out ourselves," Hannah said, her eyes fixed and determined, a flicker of the old Olivia, the one who would fearlessly dive into her art, now channeled into this terrifying reality. "Olivia wouldn't have wanted us to just sit here and be scared. She'd want us to find out what's happening. What happened to Abigail?"

Their investigation was a clandestine affair, conducted in hushed whispers and stolen moments. They scoured Olivia's room, searching for any clues she might have left behind, anything that might shed light on her final days. They found her sketchbook, filled with intricate drawings, many of them depicting a shadowy, distorted figure with long, dark hair—a figure that bore a chilling resemblance to the Abigail they remembered, or rather, the Abigail they feared. There were also unsettling sketches of distorted faces, of empty spaces, and of a pervasive darkness that seemed to consume everything.

One particular drawing caught their attention. It was a detailed rendering of the girls' restroom, the scene of Olivia's initial terrifying encounter. In the corner, half-hidden by the harsh fluorescent light, was a figure with unnaturally long, dark hair, its form indistinct, almost as if it were made of shadow. Beneath the drawing, Olivia had scrawled a single word, in shaky, desperate letters: "It sees me."

The discovery sent a fresh wave of terror through them. Olivia had known. She had been aware of the danger, of the entity that was stalking her. And the fact that she had chosen to document it, to capture it in her art, spoke volumes about her fear and her desperate attempt to understand the inexplicable.

The police, meanwhile, continued to chase down dead ends. They interviewed Abigail's parents, who were distraught and confused, insisting their daughter had been deeply troubled but hardly capable of such a heinous act. They spoke of Abigail's increasing isolation, her strange pronouncements about feeling watched, about a darkness that was closing in. But their accounts offered no concrete leads, only a growing sense of the psychological turmoil Abigail had been experiencing.

As the investigation stalled, the whispers intensified. Students who had previously dismissed the talk of Abigail as mere rumor now began to recall their own unsettling encounters, their own glimpses of the uncanny. A locker that slammed shut on its own, a chilling whisper heard when no one was around, a feeling of being watched from the empty corners of the school. These isolated incidents, once dismissed as trivial, now took on a new, sinister significance. The collective fear was palpable, a silent acknowledgment that something deeply wrong had infiltrated their community.

Hannah and Emma knew they couldn't wait for the authorities. The chilling reality of Olivia's death, the undeniable connection to Abigail, and the growing sense of dread that permeated their school were too immediate, too terrifying to ignore. They were on their own, armed with nothing but Olivia's fragmented clues and a burgeoning understanding that the horror that had claimed their friend was not of this world. The despair of Olivia's loss was a constant ache, but it was now intertwined with a desperate resolve. They had to uncover the truth, not just for Olivia, but for themselves, before the darkness that had claimed her could claim them too. The silence in the school wasn't just the silence of shock anymore; it was the silence of fear, of a shared, unspoken terror that was beginning to take root. And in that terrifying stillness, the specter of Abigail, no longer just a missing classmate, but a terrifying, vengeful force, loomed larger than ever. The discovery of Olivia's body had not brought closure, but a chilling awakening.

The weight of Olivia's absence was a physical ache in Hannah's chest, a constant, dull throb that pulsed with every beat of her heart. It had been days since the library had become a scene of unspeakable horror, days filled with the hollow drone of police inquiries and the unnerving whispers of her classmates. Yet, the shock had done little to numb the raw wound of grief. Instead, it had festered, breeding a potent cocktail of guilt and a gnawing paranoia that clung to Hannah like a second skin. Every creak of the floorboards in her bedroom, every rustle of leaves against her windowpane, sent a jolt of icy fear through her. She found herself scrutinizing every shadow, her mind a frantic reel of Olivia's last days, replaying fragmented conversations, her friend's increasingly agitated state, and the unnerving presence they had all felt emanating from Abigail.

The memory of Olivia's last text, a frantic, jumbled message about feeling watched, about her, had been dismissed by Hannah as the product of teenage anxiety, amplified by the pressures of upcoming exams and social dramas. She had been so quick to rationalize, so eager to believe in the mundane, to maintain the comforting illusion of normalcy. Now, that normalcy lay shattered, a victim of the same brutal, inexplicable force that had stolen Olivia. The sheer horror of Olivia's death—the unnatural angles of her body, the terrifyingly precise marks of strangulation that suggested a force beyond human comprehension—had irrevocably altered Hannah's perception of reality. It wasn't just a murder; it was a violation of every known law of nature. And in the echoing silence left by Olivia's absence, a terrifying theory began to take root in Hannah's mind, a theory she shared with no one, not even Emma, because it felt too monstrous, too insane to articulate.

She started to see connections, threads weaving through the fabric of their lives, sinister patterns that Olivia had, in her own way, tried to warn them about. The flickering lights in Emma's basement, the inexplicable chill that had descended upon them that night, the fleeting glimpse of Abigail's hollow eyes in the darkened window—it wasn't just a coincidence. It was a prelude. And now, Olivia was gone. Hannah found herself staring at Abigail's vacant locker, still sealed with police tape, a morbid fascination drawing her in. What had happened to Abigail after the football game? The rumors were vague, whispered accounts of a breakdown, of being taken away. But Hannah felt a chilling certainty that Abigail hadn't simply broken. Something had happened to her, something that had transformed her into something else entirely.

The days bled into one another, each dawn a fresh assault of dread. Sleep offered no respite, only a descent into fragmented nightmares where Olivia's silent screams echoed and Abigail's spectral form loomed, her eyes black voids, her touch a freezing caress. Hannah's guilt was a corrosive acid, eating away at her sanity. She replayed their last conversation, Olivia's desperate plea for help, her fear palpable even through the crackling static of the phone line. Hannah had been dismissive, preoccupied with trivialities, and now Olivia was dead. The weight of that regret was suffocating. She felt a profound sense of responsibility, a terrifying inkling that their past actions, however insignificant they might have seemed at the time, had somehow played a role in this unfolding horror.

She remembered the incident at the football game, the fleeting, almost imperceptible moment when Abigail had seemed to falter, her gaze fixed on something in the distance, a look of profound terror etched onto her face before she'd vanished into the throng. Hannah had noticed it, a prickle of unease, but had dismissed it as Abigail being Abigail—awkward, withdrawn, prone to moments of intense anxiety. Now, that unease had blossomed into a full-blown, paralyzing fear. She knew, with a certainty that chilled her to the bone, that Abigail had witnessed something, or perhaps experienced something, that had irrevocably changed her. And whatever had happened to Abigail, it had not ended with her disappearance. It had followed her, clung to her, and now, it had manifested in a way that had claimed Olivia.

The isolation Hannah felt was profound, a silent chasm that had opened between her and even her closest friends, including Emma. While they grieved together, a wall of unspoken understanding stood between them. Hannah carried the heavier burden, the dark secret that gnawed at her conscience. She believed, with an almost fanatical conviction, that Abigail's spirit, or whatever possessed it, was seeking retribution. And the knowledge that they, in some indirect way, might have contributed to the chain of events that led to Olivia's death, was a secret too terrible to share. She saw the horror in Emma's eyes, the lingering fear, but Emma's grief, while deep, was not laced with the same corrosive guilt that Hannah felt. Emma was mourning the loss of her friend; Hannah was mourning Olivia, and also wrestling with the terrifying possibility that she had, in some small, insidious way, helped to unleash the darkness that had devoured her.

Hannah's paranoia began to manifest in subtle ways. She started avoiding certain parts of the school, particularly the quiet, dimly lit corridors where she felt the most vulnerable. The library, once a haven, was now a forbidden zone, a chilling monument to Olivia's final moments. She found herself flinching at sudden noises, her gaze constantly scanning the periphery, searching for any sign of movement, any flicker of unnatural presence. The face of Abigail, as she remembered her—the quiet, almost ethereal girl who had always seemed on the verge of tears—was now superimposed with a distorted, terrifying image, a creature of shadow and malice.

She began to document her own observations, scribbling in a hidden notebook, her handwriting shaky and hurried. Each entry was a testament to her growing terror, a desperate attempt to make sense of the encroaching madness. She noted down every strange occurrence, every fleeting glimpse of movement in her peripheral vision, every unsettling dream. She pored over Olivia's sketchbook, searching for clues, for a deeper understanding of the entity that had claimed her friend. The drawings of the shadowy figure, with its elongated limbs and vacant eyes, sent shivers down her spine. They were not mere artistic expressions; they were chilling depictions of a tangible horror, a harbinger of the doom that had befallen Olivia.

One drawing, in particular, haunted her. It depicted the school hallway, and in the shadows near a row of lockers, a tall, slender figure was barely visible, its form blurred and indistinct, as if rendered in smoke. But its eyes, even in the sketch, seemed to pierce through the paper, burning with an unsettling intensity. Beneath it, Olivia had written, in a scrawling, desperate hand, "It watches from the edges." Hannah felt a visceral connection to that inscription. She, too, felt watched, not just by the eyes of her classmates who saw her grief and her fear, but by something else, something ancient and malevolent that lurked just beyond the veil of ordinary perception.

The isolation intensified when she tried to discuss her suspicions with Emma. While Emma was undoubtedly terrified and increasingly convinced that Abigail was involved, she still clung to a semblance of rational thought. She suggested that Abigail might be suffering from a severe mental illness, that the events were a tragic confluence of grief and delusion. But Hannah knew, with an unwavering conviction, that this was no mere delusion. The sheer force evident in Olivia's death, the unnaturalness of it all, pointed to something far more sinister, something that transcended the boundaries of human psychology. She felt a pang of frustration, a sense of betrayal, that Emma couldn't see what she saw, couldn't feel the chilling truth that was so blindingly obvious to her. It was as if they were speaking different languages, their shared grief unable to bridge the growing chasm of their understanding.

The silence that surrounded Abigail's disappearance and Olivia's death was no longer just the silence of shock, but a palpable, suffocating silence of fear. The whispers among the students had grown louder, more insistent. Stories of cold spots, of unseen presences, of doors slamming shut on their own, were circulating with a terrifying regularity. Hannah listened to them, her heart pounding in her chest, recognizing in their hushed, fearful accounts the echoes of her own growing dread. These weren't just rumors; they were shared experiences, confirmations that the darkness Olivia had sensed was indeed real, and it was spreading.

She found herself spending more time alone, poring over Olivia's belongings, as if hoping to find a hidden message, a secret diary, anything that would provide a definitive answer. She felt a desperate need to understand, to confront the truth, no matter how terrifying it might be. The guilt of her inaction, of her initial denial, was a constant spur, pushing her forward into the terrifying unknown. She was no longer just grieving; she was on a mission, driven by a desperate hope that she could somehow honor Olivia's memory by uncovering the truth, by confronting the entity that had stolen her life.

The fear, once a creeping sensation, had now become a constant companion, a cold dread that settled deep within her bones. She knew that Olivia's death was not an isolated incident, but the first ripple in a coming storm. And as the days passed, and the investigation continued to yield nothing but dead ends, Hannah felt an increasing sense of urgency. She was alone in her conviction, a solitary sentinel against a creeping, unseen terror. The secret she carried, the gnawing guilt, and the terrifying belief that Abigail's vengeful spirit was on the loose isolated her, pushing her further into the terrifying abyss of her own fear. She looked at Emma, at her genuine grief, and felt a pang of something akin to envy. Emma was still tethered to the world Hannah was rapidly losing her grip on. Hannah was being pulled into the darkness, and she suspected, with a chilling certainty, that she might not be able to pull herself back out. The weight of Olivia's death, and the secrets it had unearthed, was crushing her, transforming her from a grieving friend into a haunted soul, forever marked by the darkness that had descended upon Northwood High.

Chapter 4:

A Grim Reckoning

The oppressive silence of the school corridors had become a suffocating blanket for Hannah, a constant reminder of what had been lost and what she now suspected lurked just beyond the periphery of sight. Olivia's absence was a wound that refused to scab over, a raw, throbbing ache that pulsed with every beat of her heart. Days had bled into a monotonous cycle of police interviews, hushed whispers, and the suffocating weight of grief. Yet beneath the sorrow, a potent cocktail of guilt and a gnawing paranoia had taken root, clinging to Hannah like a shroud. Every creak of her bedroom floorboards, every rustle of leaves against her windowpane, sent icy tendrils of fear snaking through her. Her eyes scanned every shadow, her mind a frantic montage of Olivia's last days—fragmented conversations, her friend's increasing agitation, and the unsettling aura they had all felt emanating from Abigail.

Olivia's final text message, a garbled, frantic plea about feeling watched, about her, had been dismissed by Hannah as the product of teenage anxiety, amplified by exam stress and social drama. She had clung to the comforting illusion of normalcy, too eager to rationalize the inexplicable. Now, that normalcy lay shattered, a victim of the same brutal, incomprehensible force that had claimed Olivia. The sheer horror of Olivia's death—the unnatural angles of her body, the terrifyingly precise strangulation marks that suggested a strength far beyond human capability— had irrevocably warped Hannah's perception of reality. It wasn't just a murder; it was a violation of everything she understood about the world. And in the echoing void left by Olivia's absence, a terrifying theory began to solidify in Hannah's mind, a theory too monstrous, too insane to articulate, even to Emma.

She began to see connections, sinister threads weaving through the fabric of their lives, patterns Olivia had, in her own quiet way, tried to warn them about. The flickering lights in Emma's basement, the inexplicable chill that had descended upon them that night, the fleeting glimpse of Abigail's hollow eyes in the darkened window—these were not mere coincidences. They were the prelude. And now, Olivia was gone. Hannah found herself drawn to Abigail's locker, still sealed with police tape, a morbid fascination pulling her in. What had happened to Abigail after the football game? The rumors were vague, whispers of a breakdown, of being taken away. But Hannah felt a chilling certainty that Abigail hadn't simply broken. Something had happened to her, something that had transformed her. And whatever had happened to Abigail, it hadn't ended with her disappearance. It had followed her, clung to her, and now, it had manifested in a way that had claimed Olivia.

The days blurred into an indistinguishable haze, each dawn a fresh assault of dread. Sleep offered no respite, only a descent into fragmented nightmares where Olivia's silent screams echoed and Abigail's spectral form loomed, her eyes black voids, her touch a freezing caress. Hannah's guilt was a corrosive acid, eating away at her sanity. She replayed their last conversation, Olivia's desperate plea for help, her fear palpable even through the crackling static of the phone line. Hannah had been dismissive, preoccupied with trivialities, and now Olivia was dead. The weight of that regret was suffocating. She felt a profound sense of responsibility, a terrifying inkling that their past actions, however insignificant they might have seemed at the time, had somehow played a role in this unfolding horror.

She remembered the incident at the football game, the fleeting, almost imperceptible moment when Abigail had seemed to falter, her gaze fixed on something in the distance, a look of profound terror etched onto her face before she'd vanished into the throng. Hannah had noticed it, a prickle of unease, but had dismissed it as Abigail being Abigail—awkward, withdrawn, prone to moments of intense anxiety. Now, that unease had blossomed into a full-blown, paralyzing fear. She knew, with a certainty that chilled her to the bone, that Abigail had witnessed something, or perhaps experienced something, that had irrevocably changed her. And whatever had happened to Abigail, it had not ended with her disappearance. It had followed her, clung to her, and now, it had manifested in a way that had claimed Olivia.

The isolation Hannah felt was profound, a silent chasm that had opened between her and even her closest friends, including Emma. While they grieved together, a wall of unspoken understanding stood between them. Hannah carried the heavier burden, the dark secret that gnawed at her conscience. She believed, with an almost fanatical conviction, that Abigail's spirit, or whatever possessed it, was seeking retribution. And the knowledge that they, in some indirect way, might have contributed to the chain of events that led to Olivia's death, was a secret too terrible to share. She saw the horror in Emma's eyes, the lingering fear, but Emma's grief, while deep, was not laced with the same corrosive guilt that Hannah felt. Emma was mourning the loss of her friend; Hannah was mourning Olivia, and also wrestling with the terrifying possibility that she had, in some small, insidious way, helped to unleash the darkness that had devoured her.

Hannah's paranoia began to manifest in subtle ways. She started avoiding certain parts of the school, particularly the quiet, dimly lit corridors where she felt the most vulnerable. The library, once a haven, was now a forbidden zone, a chilling monument to Olivia's final moments. She found herself flinching at sudden noises, her gaze constantly scanning the periphery, searching for any sign of movement, any flicker of unnatural presence. The face of Abigail, as she remembered her—the quiet, almost ethereal girl who had always seemed on the verge of tears—was now superimposed with a distorted, terrifying image, a creature of shadow and malice.

She began to document her own observations, scribbling in a hidden notebook, her handwriting shaky and hurried. Each entry was a testament to her growing terror, a desperate attempt to make sense of the encroaching madness. She noted down every strange occurrence, every fleeting glimpse of movement in her peripheral vision, every unsettling dream. She pored over Olivia's sketchbook, searching for clues, for a deeper understanding of the entity that had claimed her friend. The drawings of the shadowy figure, with its elongated limbs and vacant eyes, sent shivers down her spine. They were not mere artistic expressions; they were chilling depictions of a tangible horror, a harbinger of the doom that had befallen Olivia.

One drawing, in particular, haunted her. It depicted the school hallway, and in the shadows near a row of lockers, a tall, slender figure was barely visible, its form blurred and indistinct, as if rendered in smoke. But its eyes, even in the sketch, seemed to pierce through the paper, burning with an unsettling intensity. Beneath it, Olivia had written, in a scrawling, desperate hand, "It watches from the edges." Hannah felt a visceral connection to that inscription. She, too, felt watched, not just by the eyes of her classmates who saw her grief and her fear, but by something else, something ancient and malevolent that lurked just beyond the veil of ordinary perception.

The silence that surrounded Abigail's disappearance and Olivia's death was no longer just the silence of shock, but a palpable, suffocating silence of fear. The whispers among the students had grown louder, more insistent. Stories of cold spots, of unseen presences, of doors slamming shut on their own, were circulating with a terrifying regularity. Hannah listened to them, her heart pounding in her chest, recognizing in their hushed, fearful accounts the echoes of her own growing dread. These weren't just rumors; they were shared experiences, confirmations that the darkness Olivia had sensed was indeed real, and it was spreading.

She found herself spending more time alone, poring over Olivia's belongings, as if hoping to find a hidden message, a secret diary, anything that would provide a definitive answer. She felt a desperate need to understand, to confront the truth, no matter how terrifying it might be. The guilt of her inaction, of her initial denial, was a constant spur, pushing her forward into the terrifying unknown. She was no longer just grieving; she was on a mission, driven by a desperate hope that she could somehow honor Olivia's memory by uncovering the truth, by confronting the entity that had stolen her life.

The fear, once a creeping sensation, had now become a constant companion, a cold dread that settled deep within her bones. She knew that Olivia's death was not an isolated incident, but the first ripple in a coming storm. And as the days passed, and the investigation continued to yield nothing but dead ends, Hannah felt an increasing sense of urgency. She was alone in her conviction, a solitary sentinel against a creeping, unseen terror. The secret she carried, the gnawing guilt, and the terrifying belief that Abigail's vengeful spirit was on the loose, isolated her, pushing her further into the terrifying abyss of her own fear. She looked at Emma, at her genuine grief, and felt a pang of something akin to envy. Emma was still tethered to the world Hannah was rapidly losing her grip on. Hannah was being pulled into the darkness, and she suspected, with a chilling certainty, that she might not be able to pull herself back out. The weight of Olivia's death, and the secrets it had unearthed, was crushing her, transforming her from a grieving friend into a haunted soul, forever marked by the darkness that had descended upon Northwood High.

Emily, however, remained a stubborn island of disbelief in the sea of rising panic. While the rest of Northwood High seemed to be collectively succumbing to the creeping dread, Emily actively resisted it, her defiance a brittle shield against the encroaching fear. She'd always been the pragmatist, the one who scoffed at ghost stories and attributed unexplained phenomena to faulty wiring or overactive imaginations. Olivia's death, as horrific as it was, had been initially filed away in Emily's mind under "tragic accident" or perhaps a particularly gruesome bullying incident, the details of which had been deliberately obscured. She'd attended the memorial service, her face a mask of polite sorrow, but her mind was already elsewhere, occupied with the upcoming debate club competition and the looming threat of a pop quiz in AP Calculus.

The persistent rumors, the hushed whispers of Abigail's malevolent presence, the unnerving similarities between Olivia's death and the unsettling occurrences at the football game—Emily dismissed them all as hysteria, mass delusion fueled by grief. She saw Hannah's increasingly frantic behavior, her haunted eyes and trembling hands, not as a sign of profound insight, but as further evidence of a mind unraveling under pressure. "She's losing it," Emily had confided to Sarah during lunch, her voice low and conspiratorial, as if Hannah's sanity was a commodity to be dissected and discarded. "Olivia's death was terrible, but it doesn't mean the whole school is cursed. People are just looking for something to blame, something to make sense of the senseless."

Emily's particular brand of denial wasn't born from a place of deep-seated fear, but rather from a fierce, almost aggressive need to maintain control. Her life was a carefully constructed edifice of order and predictability. Deviations from the norm were not just inconvenient; they were an affront to her very being. The idea of an unseen force, a supernatural entity with the power to inflict such devastation, was anathema to her worldview. It would mean that her meticulously planned life, her logical approach to problem-solving, her very understanding of how the world worked, was fundamentally flawed. And Emily could not, would not, accept that.

Driven by this need to assert her dominance over the burgeoning chaos, Emily decided to confront the source of the rumors head-on, or at least, what she perceived to be the source. Abigail. She wouldn't, of course, go to Abigail's house. That would be far too dramatic, too… superstitious. Instead, Emily sought out places where Abigail had been, places that, according to the whispers, held some lingering residue of her unsettling presence. Her initial target was the old, abandoned greenhouse on the edge of the school grounds, a place where Emily had once seen Abigail sitting alone, staring blankly at the cracked glass panes, a single tear tracking a silent path down her cheek. Emily remembered the incident with a shudder, the pervasive sense of unease that had settled over her even then, a feeling she'd immediately suppressed.

One blustery afternoon, armed with a defiant smirk and a carefully curated playlist of upbeat pop music designed to ward off any lingering gloom, Emily made her way to the dilapidated greenhouse. The air inside was thick with the scent of damp earth and decay, the skeletal remains of forgotten plants reaching like clawed hands towards the weak sunlight filtering through the grime-streaked glass. Dust motes danced in the shafts of light, giving the space an ethereal, almost spectral quality that Emily resolutely ignored. She walked through the decaying aisles, her boots crunching on fallen leaves and shattered terracotta, her eyes scanning the space with an air of detached curiosity.

"Alright, Abigail," she muttered to herself, her voice echoing unnervingly in the stillness. "Let's see what you've got." She half-expected a spectral manifestation, a disembodied whisper, or perhaps a sudden drop in temperature. She was, in a perverse way, almost looking forward to being proven wrong, to experiencing something that would validate her dismissal of the supernatural. It would be a story to tell, a testament to her bravery in the face of fabricated terror.

Emily found a rusted, overturned potting bench near a collapsed section of the greenhouse wall. This, she vaguely recalled, was where someone had claimed Abigail had been seen chanting or muttering to herself. Emily approached it, her movements deliberately nonchalant. She ran a hand over the pitted metal, a faint tremor in her fingers that she quickly disguised by flexing her hand. Nothing. No ghostly apparitions, no sudden chills, no whispers from the beyond. Just the pervasive smell of decay and the unsettling quiet.

"See?" she said aloud, a triumphant note in her voice. "Nothing here. Just an old, creepy greenhouse. Abigail was probably just… sad. Depressed. We all get like that sometimes." She kicked at a loose brick, enjoying the satisfying thud it made. Emily's bravado, however, was a fragile facade. As she turned to leave, a sharp, inexplicable pain shot through her ankle. She yelped, stumbling, and looked down to see that her foot had somehow become ensnared in a tangle of thick, thorny vines that seemed to have sprung from the very earth, as if animated by some unseen force. They were unlike any vines she'd seen before—dark and impossibly strong, their thorns like tiny, sharpened needles.

"What the…?" she grunted, trying to pull her foot free. The vines tightened their grip, biting into her ankle with an alarming ferocity. Panic, cold and sharp, began to prick at the edges of her carefully constructed composure. She tugged harder, her breath coming in ragged gasps. The thorns dug deeper, drawing blood. "Get off me!" she screamed, her voice cracking. The upbeat pop music playing from her earbuds suddenly seemed like a mockery of her situation, the cheerful lyrics a stark contrast to the primal terror seizing her.

In her desperate struggle, Emily's gaze fell upon a patch of disturbed earth near the base of the potting bench. There, half-buried in the dirt, was a small, tarnished silver locket. It was intricately engraved, its surface dulled by time and neglect. Emily recognized it instantly. It belonged to Olivia. She remembered seeing Olivia wear it often, a cherished keepsake, a gift from her grandmother. How had it gotten here?

Had Olivia been here? The thought sent a fresh wave of dread through Emily, a tremor of doubt that finally began to chip away at her unwavering denial.

As Emily fumbled with the clasp of the locket, trying to pry it open, a subtle shift occurred in the atmosphere of the greenhouse. The air grew heavy, charged with an unseen energy. The shadows deepened, coalescing in the corners of her vision. A low hum, almost imperceptible at first, began to emanate from the vines ensnaring her ankle. It was a discordant sound, a dissonant thrum that seemed to vibrate not just in the air, but within her very bones.

Emily finally managed to pry open the locket. Inside, instead of a photograph, were two tiny, dried flowers, pressed and fragile. As she looked at them, a wave of nausea washed over her. The flowers were wilting, their petals blackened and curled, as if consumed by an unnatural blight. And then, she heard it. Not a whisper, not a hum, but a chilling, guttural growl that seemed to emanate from the very earth beneath her feet.

Emily's eyes darted around the greenhouse, her heart hammering against her ribs. The shadows were no longer just shadows; they were shifting, coalescing into something darker, more defined. She saw it then, a fleeting, indistinct shape at the edge of her vision, a flicker of movement that was too fast, too unnatural to be anything human. It was tall, impossibly thin, with limbs that seemed to bend at wrong angles, its form wavering like heat haze. And its eyes… or where its eyes should have been, there were only dark, empty voids.

The vines around her ankle tightened further, constricting with brutal force. Emily cried out, a raw sound of pure terror. She looked at the locket in her hand, at the blighted flowers, and a horrifying realization dawned upon her. This wasn't just a random accident. This wasn't hysteria. This was Abigail. Or what Abigail had become. And by seeking her out, by touching Olivia's locket, Emily had drawn its attention. She had become a target.

Her defiance, her need for control, her stubborn refusal to acknowledge the terrifying reality that had befallen her school, had been her undoing. She had underestimated the darkness, dismissed the warnings, and in doing so, had made herself exquisitely vulnerable. Emily, who had always believed herself to be the strongest, the most rational, the most in control, was now utterly at the mercy of a force she couldn't comprehend, a force she had actively provoked.

The growl intensified, morphing into a low, rasping hiss. The shadowy figure seemed to solidify, its skeletal form outlined against the deepening gloom. Emily could feel its malevolent gaze, a chilling weight that bore down on her, stripping away any last vestige of her bravado. The vines, imbued with an unnatural strength, began to drag her down, pulling her towards the disturbed earth, towards the darkness that now seemed to seep from every corner of the greenhouse.

Her desperate struggle became a pathetic thrashing against an insurmountable force. The locket slipped from her numb fingers, falling back into the dirt, swallowed by the encroaching shadows. Emily's screams were muffled by the suffocating air, swallowed by the guttural hiss of the entity closing in. Her final moments were a blur of pain, terror, and the horrifying certainty that her stubborn disbelief had not protected her, but had instead sealed her fate, making her the next victim of the vengeful entity that haunted Northwood High. Emily's fatal mistake wasn't a single action, but a pervasive attitude: a deep-seated hubris that led her to believe she was immune to the darkness, that her own rational mind was a shield strong enough to deflect the supernatural. In her quest to disprove the unsettling reality, she had inadvertently invited it in, and it had claimed her with a brutal, unforgiving efficiency.

The familiar comfort of her bedroom, a sanctuary meticulously curated with posters of indie bands and stacks of well-worn paperbacks, had become a cage. Emily, or what was left of her, was trapped. The events in the greenhouse, the suffocating grip of those impossibly strong vines, the guttural hiss that had promised oblivion—they had all been a prelude. Now, the horror had followed her home. It had seeped through the cracks in her carefully constructed reality, breaching the fortress of her own house.

It started subtly, insidiously. A door left ajar that she distinctly remembered closing, the faint scent of damp earth and decay that clung to the air despite the open windows. Emily, ever the skeptic, had initially dismissed these anomalies. Her mind, still reeling from the trauma of the greenhouse—

a trauma she refused to articulate, even to herself—was prone to error, prone to seeing phantoms where none existed.

She was exhausted, she told herself, running on fumes and the adrenaline of a near-fatal encounter that she was determined to relegate to the realm of the improbable.

But the impossibilities multiplied. Her favorite mug, usually perched on the edge of her desk, was found meticulously placed in the center of her pillow. The pages of her physics textbook, a subject she prided herself on mastering, were turned to random, nonsensical passages, underlined with a spidery, almost childish script that was utterly alien to her own neat, precise handwriting. Each discovery chipped away at her resolve, widening the chasm between her rational mind and the undeniable evidence of something deeply wrong.

One evening, as the last vestiges of daylight bled from the sky, Emily sat in her living room, attempting to lose herself in a movie. The familiar plot, the predictable dialogue, should have been a comfort. Instead, it felt like a thin veil, easily torn by the encroaching dread. A sudden, sharp rap echoed from the front door, startling her.

Her heart leaped into her throat. It was late. No one visited unannounced, especially not after dark.

Hesitantly, she rose and crept towards the door, peering through the peephole. The street was empty, bathed in the sickly yellow glow of the streetlights. No one was there. Yet, the rapping came again, louder this time, more insistent. A tremor ran through her. It wasn't the solid, reassuring knock of a human hand. It was a series of sharp, staccato taps, like fingernails skittering across wood.

"Who's there?" she called out, her voice thin and reedy. No answer. The tapping ceased abruptly, replaced by an unnerving silence. Emily held her breath, straining to hear any sound, any indication of what, or who, was lurking just beyond the threshold. Then, she felt it – a palpable pressure against the door, as if something heavy were leaning against it from the outside. It wasn't just a physical presence; it was a psychic weight, a malevolent intent that pressed in on her, suffocating her.

Her eyes, wide with terror, darted to the door handle. It began to turn, slowly, deliberately. Emily stumbled backward, her breath catching in her chest. This was impossible. The door was locked. She had double-checked. Yet, the handle continued its agonizing rotation, a silent testament to the violation of her home, her sanctuary.

She turned and fled, a primal scream tearing from her throat, not towards the back door, but towards her bedroom, the supposed last bastion of safety. She slammed the door shut, fumbling with the lock, her fingers clumsy and slick with sweat. She leaned against the wood, her body trembling uncontrollably, the metallic taste of fear flooding her mouth.

Inside the room, the air was thick and heavy, charged with an unseen energy. The shadows in the corners seemed to deepen, to writhe with a life of their own. Her posters, once cheerful and vibrant, now seemed to leer at her, their figures distorted and menacing. A framed photo of her and Olivia, taken just weeks before, suddenly felt like a cruel mockery, a reminder of a life and a friendship irrevocably shattered.

She scrambled for her phone, her fingers desperately swiping to unlock it. She needed to call someone, anyone. Her parents were out of town. Emma… Emma was gone. The thought sent a fresh wave of panic through her. Who was left? She dialed 911, her voice a ragged whisper as she tried to explain the impossible. "There's… there's someone in my house. No, not someone… something. It's… it's not natural."

As the dispatcher's calm, professional voice filled her ear, a chilling sound cut through the static. It was a low, guttural growl, impossibly close. It wasn't coming from outside the door anymore. It was inside the room with her. Her eyes widened in horror as she saw it – a tall, impossibly thin silhouette detaching itself from the deepest shadow near her closet. It moved with a disturbing fluidity, its limbs bending at unnatural angles, its form wavering like heat haze. The growl intensified, morphing into a raspy, sibilant hiss. Emily's hand, still clutching her phone, trembled violently. The dispatcher's voice was a distant, tinny echo. "Ma'am? Can you repeat that? I can't hear you." Emily tried to speak, to scream, but only a choked sob escaped her lips. The shadowy figure glided closer, its movement unnervingly silent, like a predator stalking its prey.

She felt an intense cold radiating from it, a cold that seeped into her very bones, stealing the breath from her lungs. The air around it seemed to warp and distort, the familiar objects in her room – her desk, her bookshelf, her bed – appearing twisted and alien in its presence. She could see no discernible features, no eyes, no mouth, only a void where a face should be, a consuming emptiness that promised utter annihilation.

The vines from the greenhouse, a memory that had already become a horrifying reality, seemed to twist and writhe in her mind's eye, an extension of this encroaching darkness. She felt a phantom sensation of being ensnared, of those impossibly strong tendrils tightening around her, pulling her down, down, down into the suffocating embrace of oblivion.

Her phone slipped from her numb fingers, clattering onto the floor. The dispatcher's voice, now tinged with concern, faded into the deafening roar of fear that consumed her. The entity was almost upon her, its spectral form shimmering, its malevolent aura a palpable force that crushed her spirit. Emily squeezed her eyes shut, not in resignation, but in a desperate, futile attempt to ward off the inevitable. Her last coherent thought was of Abigail, of the desolate expression on her face in the greenhouse, of the chilling certainty that something ancient and terrible had taken root within her, transforming her into this… this thing.

The silence that followed was absolute, broken only by the soft thud of Emily's phone as it landed on the carpet. The door to her room remained ajar, the lock still turned. The shadows in the room, however, no longer seemed to hold a terrifying secret.

They were merely shadows now, for the true darkness had finally and irrevocably taken root within the heart of Emily's home, leaving behind only the chilling stillness of absence. The invasion was complete. The unseen had become the all-consuming.

The last vestiges of struggle had long since fled Emily's eyes. What remained was a stark, wide-eyed terror, a silent scream trapped behind lips that had long ceased to form coherent sound. The tendrils, impossibly strong and disturbingly sentient, were no longer mere extensions of the shadowy entity; they were the entity, and they had found their final, fatal embrace. They had peeled away from the amorphous darkness, solidifying into strands of impossibly thick, unnaturally colored hair – the same obsidian black that had been Abigail's signature, but now imbued with a pulsating, unholy life of its own.

This wasn't the gentle caress of a lover or the playful tug of a friend. This was a vise, tightening with a horrifying, organic strength that no human muscle could possibly replicate. The hair, thousands upon thousands of individual strands, had enveloped Emily, transforming her bedroom into a grotesque tableau of her own unraveling.

They clung to her like a second skin, burrowing into her flesh, weaving through her clothes, her hair, even her open mouth, silencing any hope of a final plea.

Emily's body was a canvas for this macabre artistry. The black strands coiled around her limbs, pressing them against the confines of her own bed, pinning her like a specimen under glass. Her arms were splayed, her fingers curled into rigid claws, frozen in a gesture that was part defiance, part desperate grasping for air. The hair was everywhere, a suffocating, suffocating blanket. It filled the spaces between her teeth, forcing her jaw open in a rictus of silent agony. It snaked into her nostrils, a chilling invasion that stole the very essence of breath.

The horror wasn't just in the physical constriction; it was in the profound violation. This was Abigail's essence, weaponized. It was a hatred so potent it had coalesced, given form, and now it was systematically dismantling Emily, piece by agonizing piece. Emily thrashed, a futile, desperate dance against an opponent that was as boundless as it was relentless. Her back arched, her body contorting as the hair tightened its grip, squeezing the air from her lungs in ragged, wheezing gasps. Each gasp only drew more of the black, sentient strands deeper into her being, a chilling testament to the inescapable nature of this violation.

The texture of the hair was alien, too slick, too smooth, yet with a terrifying grip that defied any attempt to dislodge it. It felt cool against her skin, a deathly chill that seeped deeper than the winter air ever could. It wasn't just a physical sensation; it was a psychic dampening, a numbing of her senses that was as terrifying as the tightening coils themselves. It was designed to erase, to absorb, to extinguish the light of her existence.

Her eyes, wide and still locked onto some unseen point of horror, began to cloud over. The pupils dilated, then constricted, a final, frantic flicker of life struggling against the encroaching darkness. The hair pressed against her eyelids, not just covering them, but somehow seeping into the delicate tissues, obscuring her vision from the inside out. The world, once filled with the familiar comforts of her bedroom, was rapidly dissolving into an inky blackness, punctuated only by the ghastly, almost luminous sheen of the supernatural hair.

The sounds of her struggle were muted, absorbed by the very substance that was ending her. Her muffled cries, her choked whimpers, were lost within the dense weave of Abigail's revenge. It was a silent massacre, a horror play performed for an audience of one – Emily herself, and perhaps, in some unseen dimension, the malevolent consciousness that had orchestrated this final, brutal act.

There was a moment, a brief, horrifying lull, where the constriction eased ever so slightly. Emily's head lolled back against the pillow, her breath coming in shallow, desperate gulps. A flicker of hope, foolish and ephemeral, sparked within her. Had it… had it given up? Was this over? But the lull was only a prelude, a cruel moment of false reprieve. The hair didn't retreat; it regrouped.

With a horrifying, unified surge, the strands tightened again, this time with a sickening, snapping sound that Emily felt resonate through her very bones. It wasn't just tightening; it was compacting. The hair was pulling her inwards, compressing her, reducing her to nothingness. Her limbs were no longer just pinned; they were being forced into unnatural positions, joints creaking and protesting against the impossible force. The delicate bones of her fingers, her wrists, her ankles, began to splinter and break, the sounds lost in the pervasive rustle of the hair. The sensation was one of being simultaneously crushed and woven into something else. The distinct form of Emily was beginning to blur, to merge with the black mass that held her captive. It was as if the hair was not just constricting her, but actively absorbing her, drawing her very essence into its own nightmarish tapestry. Her skin, once pale and flushed with terror, began to take on a dull, lifeless hue, darkening as the hair's malevolent pigment seemed to seep into her very cells.

Her mind, fractured by terror and the sheer impossibility of her situation, struggled to comprehend the horror. This was not a natural death. This was an unmaking. She was being systematically disassembled, not by an external force, but by an internal one, by something that had been a part of her, a parasite born of a twisted friendship, now fully unleashed. The memory of Abigail, her shy smile, her quiet determination, warred with the monstrous reality of what she had become, what she was now doing.

The last vestiges of light in Emily's eyes flickered and died. Not in a dramatic, cinematic way, but in a slow, deliberate fade, as if a faulty bulb were being extinguished. The pupils, already clouded, became completely opaque, reflecting nothing but the Stygian blackness that surrounded her. Her body went limp, the tremors that had wracked it finally ceasing. But the hair did not release her.

Instead, it continued its work. It pulsed, a silent, rhythmic throb that seemed to emanate from the very core of the tangled mass. The hair was not content with merely ending Emily's life; it was redecorating her, transforming her into a grotesque monument to Abigail's final, horrific victory. The strands began to rearrange themselves, weaving and twisting around Emily's motionless form, pulling and shaping her into something… else.

Her pale skin was now almost entirely obscured by the dense, black weave. Her limbs, already broken and distorted, were being further manipulated, tucked and folded into the expanding mass of hair. It was as if the hair was a living sculptor, working with morbid precision, its medium the ruined flesh and bone of its victim. Emily's once familiar bedroom was becoming a nest, a cocoon of death, woven from the very strands of vengeance.

The sheer, overwhelming finality of it was what truly broke the remaining fragments of Emily's consciousness, if any remained. There was no escape, no reprieve, no possibility of survival. She had been trapped in the greenhouse, and now, she was trapped in death, her end meticulously crafted by a hatred that transcended the physical. The image of Olivia, her vacant stare, her body unnaturally still in the dew-kissed grass, flashed through Emily's mind. Was this how it had been for her? Was this the same silent, suffocating obliteration?

The air in the room grew heavy, thick with a scent that was both cloying and metallic, the unmistakable odor of spilled blood, even though no blood was visible. It was the scent of a life force being extinguished, of something vital being consumed. The hair seemed to swell, to grow denser, as if it were feeding on Emily's dying energy. It was a parasitic bloom, drawing sustenance from her demise.

The strands, still impossibly intertwined, began to arrange themselves into a more deliberate pattern, a macabre mosaic. They formed a distinct shape, a silhouette that was horrifyingly familiar. It was the outline of a head, crowned with an impossibly long, flowing mane of black hair. And within that silhouette, where Emily's face had been, there was now only a void, a deepening shadow that seemed to absorb all light, all hope.

The hair had not just killed Emily; it had claimed her, incorporating her into its being, making her a part of its own grotesque, eternal existence. It was a chilling testament to the power of Abigail's rage, a power so absolute it could manifest in such a horrifying, tangible way. The horror was no longer a creeping dread; it was a concrete, undeniable reality, a silent testament to the fact that the nightmare of the greenhouse had followed its victims home, and that the final reckoning had arrived not with a bang, but with the soft, terrifying rustle of a million living hairs. The finality was absolute, the victory of Abigail's wrath complete, leaving behind only a chilling stillness and the horrifying implication for Hannah and Emma, who were still blissfully, tragically unaware of the darkness that had just claimed their friend.

The sterile, impersonal hum of the morgue did little to dispel the suffocating dread that clung to Hannah and Emma like a second skin. The stark white tiles and gleaming stainless steel offered no comfort, only a chilling amplification of the horror that had unfolded. Emily's body, or what was left of it, lay beneath a stark white sheet, a silent, grotesque testament to the inexplicable violence that had befallen them. The official cause of death remained elusive, a maddening "undetermined" that echoed the police's own bewildered pronouncements. But to Hannah and Emma, the truth was horrifyingly clear, written in the same impossible stillness that had claimed Olivia.

They had seen the initial photos, the ones the uniformed officers had shown them with a grim, apologetic air. The subtle bruising around Emily's throat, the faint, almost imperceptible marks that suggested an unnatural constriction, the unnerving pallor of her skin, as if all vitality had been leached from her. Now, standing a few feet away, their breath catching in their throats, they could see the full, devastating extent of it. The dark, inky stains that seemed to bloom from beneath the sheet, the unnatural rigidity of her limbs, the way her hair, still clinging to her head in an almost defiant cascade of black, seemed to possess a life of its own, even in death. It was a chilling echo of the descriptions they'd heard of Olivia's final moments, the whisper of impossibly strong hair, the sense of something ancient and vengeful at play.

Detective Miller, a man whose usual gruff demeanor was now laced with an uncharacteristic weariness, cleared his throat. "We're still piecing things together," he said, his gaze sweeping over their pale, terrified faces. "The preliminary report... it's inconclusive. No signs of forced entry. No visible wounds consistent with foul play. It's as if she just... stopped." He hesitated, then added, his voice dropping almost to a whisper, "But the similarities to Olivia Davies' case... they're hard to ignore. Too hard."

Hannah felt a cold dread coil in her stomach. The similarities. That was the polite way of putting it. The subtle, yet undeniable connection that whispered of something far more sinister than a tragic coincidence. Olivia, found lifeless in her backyard greenhouse, looking as though she'd been embraced by the very dew-kissed leaves that surrounded her. Emily, discovered in her own bed, surrounded by an unseen force that had rendered her lifeless. Both young, both connected, both seemingly victims of an impossible, silent killer. And both, they knew with a certainty that chilled them to the bone, connected to Abigail.

Emma's hand trembled as she reached out, her fingers brushing the edge of the sheet. A single, dark strand of hair, impossibly thick and unnervingly smooth, had escaped its confinement. It lay stark against the white fabric, a tangible piece of the horror that had consumed their friend. She recoiled as if burned, her eyes wide with primal fear. "It's... it's Abigail," she choked out, her voice barely audible. "It's her. She's doing this."

Miller's expression remained unreadable, but a flicker of something—perhaps annoyance, perhaps a dawning, unwelcome comprehension—crossed his face. He had heard their earlier rambling, their half-formed accusations of a shared secret, a vengeful spirit. He had chalked it up to grief, to trauma. But looking at them now, seeing the genuine terror etched into their features, the sheer, unadulterated horror in their eyes, he couldn't dismiss it so easily. He had seen too many strange things in his career, too many cases that defied logical explanation. And the sheer peculiarity of these two deaths...

Hannah's voice was steadier, though her body felt like a plucked string, vibrating with fear. "We knew Abigail. We... we were friends with her. Before. Before everything." The words felt inadequate, a gross understatement of the shared experience that bound them to Abigail, a secret that had festered and grown, a seed of guilt that had now sprouted into a horrifying reality. "She... she made a promise. A promise that if she couldn't have something, no one would." The memory, buried deep beneath layers of denial and suppressed fear, resurfaced with sickening clarity. Abigail, her eyes burning with an unsettling intensity, her voice low and menacing, speaking of eternal bonds, of shared fates, of a twisted form of possessiveness that bordered on the fanatical.

"A promise of what, exactly?" Miller pressed, his detective instincts kicking in despite the surreal nature of the conversation. He needed something concrete, something to grasp onto in this sea of inexplicable events.

Emma finally found her voice, a desperate, ragged whisper. "She said she'd make sure we never forgot her. That we'd always be… together." The horror of those words, spoken in a moment of misguided, possessive anguish by a teenage girl, now resonated with chilling, deadly accuracy. Abigail, consumed by her own pain and betrayal, had found a way to enact her revenge, a way that transcended the boundaries of life and death.

They looked at each other, Hannah and Emma, a silent, shared understanding passing between them. This wasn't random. This was targeted. Abigail's spectral fury, fueled by whatever dark forces they had inadvertently unleashed in their youth, was systematically dismantling their lives, their friendships, their very existence. The greenhouse incident, the whispered secrets, the pact they had all, in some naive and terrifying way, entered into – it had all culminated in this. Abigail was claiming her due, and her power, terrifyingly, seemed to be growing with each conquest.

"It's the hair," Hannah said, her voice firm, resolute, even as a fresh wave of panic threatened to overwhelm her. "Olivia's hair was long. Emily's… look at it." She gestured towards the sheet, her hand shaking uncontrollably. "It's too long. It's… unnatural. It's how she's doing it. She's using it." The tangible evidence, that single dark strand, felt like a damning indictment. It was Abigail's essence, twisted and weaponized, manifesting in the most horrifying way imaginable.

Miller followed her gaze, his brow furrowed. He saw it too, the unnerving length, the almost unnatural sheen. He had seen plenty of unusual things, but this… this felt different. It was the subtle, chilling wrongness that whispered of something beyond the realm of the mundane. He remembered the faint, almost imperceptible strands found near Olivia's body, dismissed as garden debris at the time. Now, they seemed to take on a sinister significance.

"We need to… we need to stop her," Emma pleaded, her voice cracking. "We don't know what she's going to do next. But she's coming for us. She's not going to stop until we're both…" She couldn't finish the sentence. The thought of her own body, rendered as lifeless and still as Emily's, was a vision that seared itself into her mind.

The weight of their shared secret pressed down on them, a suffocating burden. They had tried to outrun it, to bury it, to pretend it never happened. But Abigail's wrath was a tenacious entity, a shadow that had stretched and grown, finding them even in their most private spaces. The chilling realization that they were not merely the witnesses to a tragedy, but the intended targets of a supernatural vendetta, left them in a state of abject terror. There was no rational explanation for what was happening, no logical escape from a force that defied the laws of nature. They were trapped in a nightmare, and the only way out, they feared, was to face the darkness that had consumed their friends, and pray they weren't already too late. The police, bound by procedure and a desperate need for evidence, were fumbling in the dark, while the true horror was all too real, all too present, and all too intimate. The pattern had emerged, a terrifying tableau of Abigail's revenge, and Hannah and Emma were the only ones who truly understood its grim design. They were next.

The sterile quiet of the morgue had finally given way to the muted chaos of the outside world, but for Hannah and Emma, the silence within them was far more deafening. Emily's vacant eyes, the unnatural stillness of her limbs, the dark, impossibly long strands of hair that had been found clinging to her even after the initial examination – these were images seared into their minds, fueling a gnawing paranoia that now dictated their every breath. They were the last two. The horrifying finality of that thought settled over them like a shroud. Olivia, then Emily, and now... them. The pattern was undeniable, a terrifying trajectory pointing directly at their own fragile lives. It was a grim reckoning, not just for the friends they had lost, but for the choices they had made, the secrets they had kept, and the Pandora's Box they had unwittingly, or perhaps not so unwittingly, opened.

Their friendship, once a bedrock of shared laughter and unwavering support, now felt like a precariously balanced structure, constantly threatening to crumble under the immense pressure of their shared trauma and guilt. Every glance, every whispered word, was laced with an unspoken fear. Had they done enough? Had they ever done enough? The weight of their complicity, the knowledge that their youthful recklessness had unleashed something ancient and vengeful, pressed down on them with suffocating intensity. They were no longer just grieving friends; they were survivors, burdened with a knowledge so profound and so terrifying that it alienated them from the rest of the world. The casual concerns of their peers, the mundane worries of school and social lives, felt impossibly distant, like echoes from another planet. How could they possibly explain the chilling whispers in the dark, the phantom touch of impossibly long hair, the unshakeable certainty that they were being hunted by something that had once been their friend?

The isolation was absolute, a vast, echoing chasm that separated them from everyone else. Detective Miller, bless his weary, rational soul, was trying. He was dutifully following the leads, scrutinizing forensic reports, and attempting to make sense of the senseless. But even he, with his years of experience in the darker corners of human behavior, couldn't grasp the true nature of the horror they faced. To him, it was a series of tragic, albeit bizarre, deaths. To Hannah and Emma, it was relentless, supernatural retribution.

They saw the flicker of disbelief in his eyes when they spoke of Abigail, of her promises, of the unnatural hair. He saw grief, he saw trauma, he saw two young women clinging to a shared delusion. But he didn't see the malevolent force that watched them, waiting, growing stronger with each fallen friend. This deep-seated inability of anyone else to truly comprehend their reality forged an almost desperate reliance on each other. They were the only two people in the world who understood the unspeakable truth, the only ones who could truly see the spectral hand pulling the strings.

This shared burden, however, was a double-edged sword. It was their only solace, but it was also a constant reminder of their precarious position. Hannah found herself scrutinizing Emma's every move, every expression. Was that a flicker of doubt in her eyes, or just exhaustion? Was her laughter genuine, or a desperate attempt to hold onto normalcy? The paranoia gnawed at her, whispering insidious doubts. What if Emma couldn't handle it? What if she broke? The thought of being truly alone, of facing Abigail's wrath without even one ally, sent a fresh wave of icy terror through her veins. Conversely, she saw the same fear reflected in Emma's own gaze, the same desperate plea for reassurance.

They were trapped in a feedback loop of fear, each looking to the other for strength, but finding only a reflection of their own vulnerability. Their conversations became clipped, guarded, punctuated by long silences filled with the unspoken horrors that haunted them. They spoke in hushed tones, always scanning their surroundings, always listening for the phantom rustle of leaves or the almost imperceptible whisper of a name on the wind. Every shadow seemed to lengthen, every creak of the floorboards sounded like a footstep. Sleep offered no respite, only a different kind of terror, filled with nightmares of dark, impossibly long hair wrapping around them, suffocating them, pulling them into an abyss from which there was no escape.

The weight of their actions, the pact they had made—however foolishly, however unknowingly—in the sun-dappled innocence of their youth, now felt like a colossal burden of sin. They remembered Abigail's words, her desperate pronouncements of ownership, her chilling threats. At the time, they had dismissed them as the ramblings of a heartbroken, unstable girl. Now, those words echoed with terrifying, prophetic clarity. She had promised they would never forget her, that they would always be together. And in the most horrific way imaginable, she was making good on that promise. Abigail, or whatever dark entity had taken root within her, was systematically erasing them from the world, leaving behind only the chilling remnants of her rage.

They were left with the devastating realization that their youthful indiscretion, their attempt to dabble in forces they didn't understand, had not only cost them their friends but had now put their own lives on the line. There was no escaping the consequences, no hiding from the reckoning. They were irrevocably bound to Abigail's fate, and her vengeful spirit was determined to drag them down with her.

The burden of survival was not just about staying alive; it was about living with the knowledge of what they had done, and the terrifying understanding that they were the last vestiges of a shared, damning secret. They were the living embodiment of Abigail's unfinished business, and their survival depended on deciphering the twisted logic of her wrath before it consumed them entirely.

Chapter 5:

Desperate Measures

The sterile quiet of the morgue had finally given way to the muted chaos of the outside world, but for Hannah and Emma, the silence within them was far more deafening. Emily's vacant eyes, the unnatural stillness of her limbs, the dark, impossibly long strands of hair that had been found clinging to her even after the initial examination—these were images seared into their minds, fueling a gnawing paranoia that now dictated their every breath. They were the last two. The horrifying finality of that thought settled over them like a shroud. Olivia, then Emily, and now… them. The pattern was undeniable, a terrifying trajectory pointing directly at their own fragile lives. It was a grim reckoning, not just for the friends they had lost, but for the choices they had made, the secrets they had kept, and the Pandora's Box they had unwittingly, or perhaps not so unwittingly, opened.

Their friendship, once a bedrock of shared laughter and unwavering support, now felt like a precariously balanced structure, constantly threatening to crumble under the immense pressure of their shared trauma and guilt. Every glance, every whispered word, was laced with an unspoken fear. Had they done enough? Had they ever done enough? The weight of their complicity, the knowledge that their youthful recklessness had unleashed something ancient and vengeful, pressed down on them with suffocating intensity. They were no longer just grieving friends; they were survivors, burdened with a knowledge so profound and so terrifying that it alienated them from the rest of the world. The casual concerns of their peers, the mundane worries of school and social lives, felt impossibly distant, like echoes from another planet. How could they possibly explain the chilling whispers in the dark, the phantom touch of impossibly long hair, the unshakeable certainty that they were being hunted by something that had once been their friend?

The isolation was absolute, a vast, echoing chasm that separated them from everyone else. Detective Miller, bless his weary, rational soul, was trying. He was dutifully following the leads, scrutinizing forensic reports, and attempting to make sense of the senseless. But even he, with his years of experience in the darker corners of human behavior, couldn't grasp the true nature of the horror they faced. To him, it was a series of tragic, albeit bizarre, deaths. To Hannah and Emma, it was relentless, supernatural retribution. They saw the flicker of disbelief in his eyes when they spoke of Abigail, of her promises, of the unnatural hair. He saw grief, he saw trauma, he saw two young women clinging to a shared delusion. But he didn't see the malevolent force that watched them, waiting, growing stronger with each fallen friend.

This deep-seated inability of anyone else to truly comprehend their reality forged an almost desperate reliance on each other. They were the only two people in the world who understood the unspeakable truth, the only ones who could truly see the spectral hand pulling the strings. This shared burden, however, was a double-edged sword. It was their only solace, but it was also a constant reminder of their precarious position.

Hannah found herself scrutinizing Emma's every move, every expression. Was that a flicker of doubt in her eyes, or just exhaustion? Was her laughter genuine, or a desperate attempt to hold onto normalcy? The paranoia gnawed at her, whispering insidious doubts. What if Emma couldn't handle it? What if she broke? The thought of being truly alone, of facing Abigail's wrath without even one ally, sent a fresh wave of icy terror through her veins. Conversely, she saw the same fear reflected in Emma's own gaze, the same desperate plea for reassurance. They were trapped in a feedback loop of fear, each looking to the other for strength, but finding only a reflection of their own vulnerability.

Their conversations became clipped, guarded, punctuated by long silences filled with the unspoken horrors that haunted them. They spoke in hushed tones, always scanning their surroundings, always listening for the phantom rustle of leaves or the almost imperceptible whisper of a name on the wind. Every shadow seemed to lengthen, every creak of the floorboards sounded like a footstep. Sleep offered no respite, only a different kind of terror, filled with nightmares of dark, impossibly long hair wrapping around them, suffocating them, pulling them into an abyss from which there was no escape.

The weight of their actions, the pact they had made—however foolishly, however unknowingly—in the sun-dappled innocence of their youth, now felt like a colossal burden of sin. They remembered Abigail's words, her desperate pronouncements of ownership, her chilling threats. At the time, they had dismissed them as the ramblings of a heartbroken, unstable girl. Now, those words echoed with a terrifying, prophetic clarity. She had promised they would never forget her, that they would always be together. And in the most horrific way imaginable, she was making good on that promise. Abigail, or whatever dark entity had taken root within her, was systematically erasing them from the world, leaving behind only the chilling remnants of her rage. They were left with the devastating realization that their youthful indiscretion, their attempt to dabble in forces they didn't understand, had not only cost them their friends but had now put their own lives on the line. There was no escaping the consequences, no hiding from the reckoning. They were irrevocably bound to Abigail's fate, and her vengeful spirit was determined to drag them down with her. The burden of survival was not just about staying alive; it was about living with the knowledge of what they had done, and the terrifying understanding that they were the last vestiges of a shared, damning secret. They were the living embodiment of Abigail's unfinished business, and their survival depended on deciphering the twisted logic of her wrath before it consumed them entirely.

The finality of Emily's death had been a brutal, unassailable truth. The police tape, the hushed, grim pronouncements from the paramedics, the sheer emptiness that had settled over the scene—it had all coalesced into a truth too horrific to bear. Hannah had watched Emma's face, saw the stark terror bloom in her eyes, the way her breath hitched, and knew, with a certainty that chilled her to the bone, that the whispered, desperate pact made weeks ago under the indifferent gaze of the moon was no longer a foolish, youthful indiscretion. It was their only lifeline. The authorities, bless their well-meaning but utterly clueless hearts, were chasing ghosts in the daylight. They spoke of toxicology reports, of accidental overdoses, of tragic, isolated incidents.

They saw the shattered remnants of grief and guilt in Hannah and Emma, the two sole survivors, and attributed their mounting terror to post-traumatic stress. They couldn't see the tendrils of dark energy, the suffocating presence that clung to them like grave dust, the way Abigail's vengeful spirit, or whatever it had become, was a predator, and they were its prey.

"They can't help us, Em," Hannah had said, her voice barely a whisper, the words feeling like grit on her tongue. They were huddled in Hannah's bedroom, the curtains drawn tight against the encroaching dusk, as if by shutting out the world, they could also shut out the horror that pursued them. Emily's phone, still clutched in Hannah's hand, felt like a death knell, a stark reminder of the unanswered calls, the desperate attempts to warn her, to protect her. It was a futile gesture now, a haunting monument to their failure.

Emma nodded, her eyes wide and unfocused, staring at a point somewhere beyond the peeling wallpaper of Hannah's room. The vibrant, carefree girl who had laughed freely only months ago seemed like a distant memory, a casualty of something far older and more terrible than any of them could have imagined. "Miller… he kept asking about Abigail. About… us. About what happened at the lake." Her voice trembled, each syllable a tiny shard of glass. "He doesn't believe us, Hannah. Not really. He thinks we're…"

"Crazy?" Hannah finished for her, a bitter laugh escaping her lips. It was a hollow sound, devoid of any humor. "He thinks we're just two girls who lost their friends. He can't comprehend that our friends were taken. That something ancient and hungry is feeding on our… our connection." She gestured vaguely between them, the air between them thick with unspoken dread. "We told him about the hair, Em. About how Emily's was like that too, just like Olivia's was described. He just looked at us. Like we were babbling."

"He thinks we're making it up. To cope," Emma added, her voice barely audible. She hugged herself, her knuckles white. "But we're not. Are we?" It wasn't a question seeking reassurance, but a desperate plea for confirmation of the horrifying reality they both shared.

Hannah met her gaze, her own eyes burning with a mixture of terror and a nascent, desperate resolve. This was it. The precipice. They could either succumb to the paralyzing fear, wait for the inevitable knock on the door, the phantom touch on their shoulder, the final, suffocating embrace of whatever Abigail had become, or they could fight back. And fighting back meant abandoning the fragile hope that someone else would save them. It meant taking their survival into their own hands.

"No," Hannah said, her voice gaining a steelier edge. "We're not making it up. And if Miller can't see it, if no one else can, then it's up to us. It has to be." She took a shaky breath, the air in the room suddenly feeling heavy, charged with an unseen energy. "We have to go to her, Em."

The words hung in the air, heavy with their implication. Go to Abigail. Confront the darkness that had consumed their friend, the entity that now seemed to hold their lives in its spectral grip. It was an insane notion, a suicidal undertaking. But the alternative was to wait for death, to be plucked off one by one like withered flowers.

Emma flinched, as if the very suggestion had physically struck her. Her eyes widened further, a raw, unadulterated terror surfacing. "Go to… her? Hannah, are you crazy? What are you talking about?"

"Think about it, Em. What else can we do?" Hannah's voice was urgent, almost pleading. "We've tried telling people. We've tried waiting. It's not working. It's making it worse. Every day that passes, it gets closer. It's like… like it's tethered to us. To what we did. To the ritual." The memory of that day, the seemingly innocent attempt to mend a friendship, to feel powerful, to dabble in something they didn't understand, was a constant, gnawing ache in her gut. The hushed chanting, the flickering candles, the strange symbols drawn in chalk on the forest floor—it all seemed so distant, so naive, yet so irrevocably tied to the horrors they faced now.

"The ritual…" Emma whispered, her gaze dropping to her hands, now twisting a loose thread on her jeans. "We just wanted to help her. We didn't know…"

"I know," Hannah interrupted, her voice softening slightly. "We were kids. We were stupid. But now we have to fix it. Or at least… survive it." She moved closer, sitting on the edge of Emma's bed, the worn quilt a stark contrast to the icy dread that permeated their shared space. "If Abigail… if this thing… wants us, then maybe we can confront it. Maybe we can find out what it wants. What she wants. And maybe, just maybe, we can bargain with it. Or… or fight it."

"Bargain?" Emma scoffed, the sound brittle. "With a monster? Hannah, Emily is dead! Olivia is dead! They're gone! And you think we can just… have a chat with whatever did this to them?"

"What choice do we have?" Hannah's voice rose, a desperate edge creeping in. "We can't keep hiding. We can't keep waiting for the next phone call, the next body. We're the only ones left who understand. The only ones who saw it coming, even if we didn't understand it then. This is our fight, Em. Ours alone." She reached out, her hand hovering for a moment before she gently covered Emma's trembling ones. "We have to be brave, Em. For Olivia. For Emily. For ourselves."

Emma finally looked up, her eyes filled with a raw, primal fear that mirrored Hannah's own. But beneath the terror, a flicker of something else ignited—a stubborn refusal to be extinguished, a desperate glimmer of defiance. The sheer weight of their shared trauma, the intimate knowledge of each other's deepest fears, had forged a bond stronger than any they had ever known. This was not just about survival; it was about a mutual responsibility, a terrifying solidarity.

"How?" Emma's voice was a raspy whisper, laced with a newfound, desperate resolve. "How do we even… find her? Find it?"

Hannah's mind raced, replaying the fragmented memories, the chilling whispers, the unnerving sensations that had followed them since that fateful day. The lake. Abigail's home. The woods where they had performed their ill-fated ritual. The places where their shared secret had been born, and where, it seemed, their fate was now inextricably linked. "Abigail's house," Hannah said, the words solidifying into a plan. "We start there. That's where it all… began. She always felt connected to that place. And the woods behind it… that's where we were."

A shiver ran through Emma's frame, but she didn't pull her hands away. Instead, she squeezed Hannah's in return, a silent acknowledgment of their shared descent into madness, their desperate pact. "What if… what if it's waiting for us there?"

"Then we face it," Hannah said, her gaze unwavering. "We face it together. We're not alone, Em. We have each other. And that's more than Olivia and Emily had in the end." The words were meant to be a comfort, but they hung in the air with a grim finality.

They were the last ones standing, the keepers of a terrible secret, and their only hope lay in confronting the very darkness that had extinguished the lives of their friends.

The fear was a suffocating blanket, but the desperate need to survive, to understand, and perhaps, in some twisted way, to avenge, was beginning to outweigh it. This was not a plan born of courage, but of sheer, unadulterated terror. A dangerous alliance, forged in the crucible of grief and the chilling certainty that their own time was running out. They were walking into the jaws of the beast, armed with nothing but their shared trauma and a desperate, terrifying hope.

The suffocating silence of Hannah's bedroom had become a tangible entity, pressing in on them, amplifying every rustle of leaves outside, every distant siren. The decision, spoken in hushed, trembling tones, had been made: they would confront Abigail's past, and in doing so, confront their own. The idea of exhuming her body was born from a desperate, almost primal need to understand, to find some tangible link to the horror that had consumed their lives. It was a mad, unspeakable act, born of unspeakable terror, but it felt like their only recourse.

Under the cloak of a moonless, starless sky, they slipped out of Hannah's house, the familiar suburban street transformed into a landscape of shadowed terrors. Each creak of a porch swing, each distant bark of a dog, sent jolts of adrenaline through them, their senses on high alert. The air was thick and heavy, carrying the damp, earthy scent of impending rain, a fittingly morbid soundtrack to their clandestine mission. They moved in a hurried, almost desperate silence, their footsteps muffled by the dew-laden grass. The weight of their undertaking pressed down on them, a physical manifestation of their guilt and fear.

The cemetery gates loomed like skeletal jaws against the ink-black sky. Hannah clutched Emma's hand, her knuckles white. The familiar ironwork, usually a symbol of quiet finality, now seemed to writhe with an unseen, malevolent energy. They squeezed through a gap in the wrought-iron fence, the metal cold and unforgiving against their skin. The path ahead was barely visible, a faint gray ribbon winding through a silent city of the dead. Rows upon rows of headstones stood like stark, unblinking sentinels, each one a silent testament to lives lived and lost.

As they ventured deeper, the oppressive silence of the cemetery began to warp, taking on a life of its own. The rustling of unseen creatures in the undergrowth sounded like hushed whispers, the sighing wind through the ancient oak trees like mournful cries. Hannah's heart hammered against her ribs, a frantic drumbeat against the unsettling stillness. She could feel Emma's trembling beside her, a mirror of her own internal turmoil. Every shadow seemed to stretch and contort, conjuring fleeting images of what they were so desperately trying to escape. The image of Abigail, her eyes once sparkling with life, now vacant and unsettlingly still, flashed behind Hannah's eyelids, fueling her resolve. This was Abigail's resting place, but it felt more like a cage, a place of confinement for something that refused to stay buried.

They reached Abigail's grave, marked by a simple, unadorned headstone. The earth around it was undisturbed, a cruel mockery of the upheaval that had shattered their lives. The sheer finality of it, the cold stone bearing Abigail's name, was almost too much to bear. This was where their friend, their confidante, lay, and yet, Hannah felt a chilling certainty that the Abigail they had known was no longer here. Something else had taken root, something that had reached out from this very spot to ensnare their other friends.

Pulling on thick work gloves, they began to dig. The spades, borrowed from Hannah's father's shed, felt heavy and unwieldy in their trembling hands. The sound of the metal biting into the earth was jarringly loud in the stillness, each scrape and thud echoing through the silent graveyard. It felt like a sacrilege, a violation of the most profound kind, yet they were driven by a desperate need to unearth the truth, to find any clue, any tangible evidence of what was happening. With every shovelful of soil they removed, they were digging themselves deeper into a forbidden past, confronting the consequences of their youthful curiosity and the dark bargain they had unknowingly struck. The earth was cool and damp, clinging to the spades, a stark reminder of the life that had once occupied this space and the unnatural stillness that now resided within it.

Hannah paused, the spade clutched in her hand, her breath catching in her throat. The air around Abigail's grave felt perceptibly colder, charged with an almost palpable energy. It was a sensation that had become all too familiar, a lingering miasma that clung to them like grave dust, a constant, unnerving reminder of the entity that had taken Abigail and was now hunting them. She glanced at Emma, whose face was pale and etched with a terror that mirrored her own.

"Do you feel that?" Hannah whispered, her voice barely audible above the thudding of her own heart.

Emma nodded, her eyes wide and fixed on the disturbed earth. "It's… it's like the air is heavy. Like something's watching."

The fear was a living, breathing thing, coiling in their stomachs, making their hands shake. Every instinct screamed at them to run, to flee this desecrated ground and the dark secrets it held. But the memory of Olivia's vacant stare, of Emily's unnaturally long hair, was a potent, agonizing reminder of what awaited them if they didn't push forward. They were trapped between the terror of this moment and the even greater terror of what lay ahead if they didn't uncover the truth. This act, this desperate digging into the past, was their only hope of finding a way to sever the invisible threads that bound them to Abigail's fate, to the darkness that had claimed her and was now relentlessly pursuing them.

They continued to dig, their movements growing more frantic with each passing moment. The hole deepened, and the weight of the earth they had displaced felt immense, mirroring the crushing burden of their shared secret. The mundane act of excavation had become a battle against an unseen force, a primal struggle against the consequences of their actions. The cloying scent of disturbed soil mingled with an almost imperceptible, yet deeply unsettling, floral fragrance—a scent Hannah vaguely recognized, a scent that had always been associated with Abigail, with her unnervingly perfect, dark hair. It was a scent that now carried the chilling undertones of decay and something far more ancient and sinister.

As they dug deeper, the wooden planks of the coffin began to emerge from the earth. The sight sent a fresh wave of nausea through Hannah. This was it. The tangible evidence of their transgression. The wood was dark, damp, and seemed to absorb the faint ambient light. It was a stark, brutal reminder of Abigail's physical presence, and the terrifying question of what lay beneath it. The air around the open grave seemed to thicken, growing colder still. The silence was no longer just an absence of sound; it was a heavy, expectant presence, as if the very ground was holding its breath, waiting.

Emma let out a choked sob, her spade clattering against the coffin lid. Her face was a mask of pure horror. "Hannah… I can't. I can't look."

Hannah reached out, her own hands shaking, and placed them on Emma's shoulders. "We have to, Em. We have to see. We need to know." Her voice was strained, barely holding back a scream. She understood Emma's terror. The thought of what they might find, of what Abigail might have become, was a terrifying abyss. But the paralyzing grip of fear was slowly being supplanted by a desperate, grim determination. They had come this far. They couldn't turn back now, not when their lives, and the memory of their lost friends, depended on what lay beneath this decaying wood. This act of desecration, however horrific, felt like the only way to reclaim some semblance of control, to confront the source of their torment head-on.

With a shared, silent understanding, they worked together, their movements clumsy and desperate, to pry open the coffin. The wood groaned in protest, a mournful sound that seemed to echo the anguish of their souls. The hinges, rusted and brittle, finally gave way, and the lid creaked open, revealing the darkness within. The floral scent intensified, cloying and sickly sweet, almost suffocating. As their eyes adjusted to the oppressive gloom, they both gasped, a strangled, involuntary sound that ripped through the oppressive silence of the cemetery. What they saw was not the peaceful slumber of the deceased, but a horrifying testament to the unnatural forces that had been at play, a chilling confirmation of their deepest fears. The darkness within the coffin was not merely the absence of light; it was a palpable entity, a void that seemed to absorb even the faintest glimmer, and from within that void, something was stirring. The long, dark strands of hair, impossibly long and impossibly dark, were more prevalent than they had imagined, matted and clinging to the still, pale form within. It was the same unsettling, unnatural hair that had been found on Olivia and Emily, a terrifying signature of the entity that had claimed Abigail. This was not just a grave; it was a gateway.

The stench of decaying earth and something sickly sweet, like overripe flowers left to rot in the sun, filled the air. It was Abigail's signature scent, the one Hannah had associated with her friend's perpetually perfect hair, her vibrant dresses, and now, it was the smell of her own undoing. Emma gagged beside her, her face ashen, her eyes wide with a terror that went beyond simple revulsion. What lay within the opened coffin wasn't just the physical remains of their friend; it was a corrupted effigy, a vessel for something ancient and malevolent. The hair, that impossibly long, inky black hair that had adorned Olivia and Emily, was there, too. It lay in thick, tangled ropes, some strands clinging to the skeletal remains, others fanning out into the depths of the coffin like grasping tendrils. It was an impossible sight, a visceral confirmation of their darkest fears. This wasn't just a grave; it was a nexus, a point of origin for the horror that had stalked their small town, a horror they had inadvertently unleashed.

Hannah forced herself to look, her stomach churning, her breath ragged. Abigail's face, what remained of it, was a gaunt, skeletal mask. Her eyes were gone, leaving hollow, cavernous sockets that seemed to stare into the very core of Hannah's soul. Yet, there was a life in those empty spaces, a furious, ancient sentience that chilled Hannah to the bone. It was Abigail's anger, magnified a thousandfold, a burning resentment that had festered for years, perhaps centuries, waiting for an opportune moment to manifest. The air around the open grave grew heavy, thick with an oppressive energy that pressed down on them, stealing their breath. It was a tangible weight, a spectral shroud woven from Abigail's fury and the dark power that had claimed her.

"She's... she's still here," Emma whispered, her voice a dry rasp. She stumbled back, tripping over a discarded shovelful of earth, her hands flying to her mouth as if to stifle a scream that threatened to erupt. The sound of her fall seemed to awaken something within the coffin, a subtle shift, a rustle of the unnatural hair that made Hannah's skin crawl. It was more than a disturbance of the dead; it was a stirring of the predatory. The very ground beneath them felt unstable, as if the earth itself was a thin veneer over an abyss of unspeakable darkness.

A shiver ran through Emma's frame, but she didn't pull her hands away. Instead, she squeezed Hannah's in return, a silent acknowledgment of their shared descent into madness, their desperate pact. "What if... what if it's waiting for us there?"

"Then we face it," Hannah said, her gaze unwavering. "We face it together. We're not alone, Em. We have each other. And that's more than Olivia and Emily had in the end." The words were meant to be a comfort, but they hung in the air with a grim finality.

They were the last ones standing, the keepers of a terrible secret, and their only hope lay in confronting the very darkness that had extinguished the lives of their friends.

The fear was a suffocating blanket, but the desperate need to survive, to understand, and perhaps, in some twisted way, to avenge, was beginning to outweigh it. This was not a plan born of courage, but of sheer, unadulterated terror. A dangerous alliance, forged in the crucible of grief and the chilling certainty that their own time was running out. They were walking into the jaws of the beast, armed with nothing but their shared trauma and a desperate, terrifying hope.

The suffocating silence of Hannah's bedroom had become a tangible entity, pressing in on them, amplifying every rustle of leaves outside, every distant siren. The decision, spoken in hushed, trembling tones, had been made: they would confront Abigail's past, and in doing so, confront their own. The idea of exhuming her body was born from a desperate, almost primal need to understand, to find some tangible link to the horror that had consumed their lives. It was a mad, unspeakable act, born of unspeakable terror, but it felt like their only recourse.

Under the cloak of a moonless, starless sky, they slipped out of Hannah's house, the familiar suburban street transformed into a landscape of shadowed terrors. Each creak of a porch swing, each distant bark of a dog, sent jolts of adrenaline through them, their senses on high alert. The air was thick and heavy, carrying the damp, earthy scent of impending rain, a fittingly morbid soundtrack to their clandestine mission. They moved in a hurried, almost desperate silence, their footsteps muffled by the dew-laden grass. The weight of their undertaking pressed down on them, a physical manifestation of their guilt and fear.

The cemetery gates loomed like skeletal jaws against the ink-black sky. Hannah clutched Emma's hand, her knuckles white. The familiar ironwork, usually a symbol of quiet finality, now seemed to writhe with an unseen, malevolent energy. They squeezed through a gap in the wrought-iron fence, the metal cold and unforgiving against their skin. The path ahead was barely visible, a faint grey ribbon winding through a silent city of the dead. Rows upon rows of headstones stood like stark, unblinking sentinels, each one a silent testament to lives lived and lost.

As they ventured deeper, the oppressive silence of the cemetery began to warp, taking on a life of its own. The rustling of unseen creatures in the undergrowth sounded like hushed whispers, the sighing wind through the ancient oak trees like mournful cries. Hannah's heart hammered against her ribs, a frantic drumbeat against the unsettling stillness. She could feel Emma's trembling beside her, a mirror of her own internal turmoil. Every shadow seemed to stretch and contort, conjuring fleeting images of what they were so desperately trying to escape. The image of Abigail, her eyes once sparkling with life, now vacant and unsettlingly still, flashed behind Hannah's eyelids, fueling her resolve. This was Abigail's resting place, but it felt more like a cage, a place of confinement for something that refused to stay buried.

They reached Abigail's grave, marked by a simple, unadorned headstone. The earth around it was undisturbed, a cruel mockery of the upheaval that had shattered their lives. The sheer finality of it, the cold stone bearing Abigail's name, was almost too much to bear. This was where their friend, their confidante, lay, and yet, Hannah felt a chilling certainty that the Abigail they had known was no longer here. Something else had taken root, something that had reached out from this very spot to ensnare their other friends.

Pulling on thick work gloves, they began to dig. The spades, borrowed from Hannah's father's shed, felt heavy and unwieldy in their trembling hands. The sound of the metal biting into the earth was jarringly loud in the stillness, each scrape and thud echoing through the silent graveyard. It felt like a sacrilege, a violation of the most profound kind, yet they were driven by a desperate need to unearth the truth, to find any clue, any tangible evidence of what was happening. With every shovelful of soil they removed, they were digging themselves deeper into a forbidden past, confronting the consequences of their youthful curiosity and the dark bargain they had unknowingly struck. The earth was cool and damp, clinging to the spades, a stark reminder of the life that had once occupied this space and the unnatural stillness that now resided within it.

Hannah paused, the spade clutched in her hand, her breath catching in her throat. The air around Abigail's grave felt perceptibly colder, charged with an almost palpable energy. It was a sensation that had become all too familiar, a lingering miasma that clung to them like grave dust, a constant, unnerving reminder of the entity that had taken Abigail and was now hunting them. She glanced at Emma, whose face was pale and etched with a terror that mirrored her own.

"Do you feel that?" Hannah whispered, her voice barely audible above the thudding of her own heart.

Emma nodded, her eyes wide and fixed on the disturbed earth. "It's… it's like the air is heavy. Like something's watching."

The fear was a living, breathing thing, coiling in their stomachs, making their hands shake. Every instinct screamed at them to run, to flee this desecrated ground and the dark secrets it held. But the memory of Olivia's vacant stare, of Emily's unnaturally long hair, was a potent, agonizing reminder of what awaited them if they didn't push forward. They were trapped between the terror of this moment and the even greater terror of what lay ahead if they didn't uncover the truth. This act, this desperate digging into the past, was their only hope of finding a way to sever the invisible threads that bound them to Abigail's fate, to the darkness that had claimed her and was now relentlessly pursuing them.

They continued to dig, their movements growing more frantic with each passing moment. The hole deepened, and the weight of the earth they had displaced felt immense, mirroring the crushing burden of their shared secret. The mundane act of excavation had become a battle against an unseen force, a primal struggle against the consequences of their actions. The cloying scent of disturbed soil mingled with an almost imperceptible, yet deeply unsettling, floral fragrance—a scent Hannah vaguely recognized, a scent that had always been associated with Abigail, with her unnervingly perfect, dark hair. It was a scent that now carried the chilling undertones of decay and something far more ancient and sinister.

As they dug deeper, the wooden planks of the coffin began to emerge from the earth. The sight sent a fresh wave of nausea through Hannah. This was it. The tangible evidence of their transgression. The wood was dark, damp, and seemed to absorb the faint ambient light. It was a stark, brutal reminder of Abigail's physical presence, and the terrifying question of what lay beneath it. The air around the open grave seemed to thicken, growing colder still. The silence was no longer just an absence of sound; it was a heavy, expectant presence, as if the very ground was holding its breath, waiting.

Emma let out a choked sob, her spade clattering against the coffin lid. Her face was a mask of pure horror. "Hannah… I can't. I can't look."

Hannah reached out, her own hands shaking, and placed them on Emma's shoulders. "We have to, Em. We have to see. We need to know." Her voice was strained, barely holding back a scream. She understood Emma's terror. The thought of what they might find, of what Abigail might have become, was a terrifying abyss. But the paralyzing grip of fear was slowly being supplanted by a desperate, grim determination. They had come this far. They couldn't turn back now, not when their lives, and the memory of their lost friends, depended on what lay beneath this decaying wood. This act of desecration, however horrific, felt like the only way to reclaim some semblance of control, to confront the source of their torment head-on.

With a shared, silent understanding, they worked together, their movements clumsy and desperate, to pry open the coffin. The wood groaned in protest, a mournful sound that seemed to echo the anguish of their souls. The hinges, rusted and brittle, finally gave way, and the lid creaked open, revealing the darkness within. The floral scent intensified, cloying and sickly sweet, almost suffocating. As their eyes adjusted to the oppressive gloom, they both gasped, a strangled, involuntary sound that ripped through the oppressive silence of the cemetery. What they saw was not the peaceful slumber of the deceased, but a horrifying testament to the unnatural forces that had been at play, a chilling confirmation of their deepest fears. The darkness within the coffin was not merely the absence of light; it was a palpable entity, a void that seemed to absorb even the faintest glimmer, and from within that void, something was stirring. The long, dark strands of hair, impossibly long and impossibly dark, were more prevalent than they had imagined, matted and clinging to the still, pale form within. It was the same unsettling, unnatural hair that had been found on Olivia and Emily, a terrifying signature of the entity that had claimed Abigail. This was not just a grave; it was a gateway.

The stench of decaying earth and something sickly sweet, like overripe flowers left to rot in the sun, filled the air. It was Abigail's signature scent, the one Hannah had associated with her friend's perpetually perfect hair, her vibrant dresses, and now, it was the smell of her own undoing. Emma gagged beside her, her face ashen, her eyes wide with a terror that went beyond simple revulsion. What lay within the opened coffin wasn't just the physical remains of their friend; it was a corrupted effigy, a vessel for something ancient and malevolent. The hair, that impossibly long, inky black hair that had adorned Olivia and Emily, was there, too. It lay in thick, tangled ropes, some strands clinging to the skeletal remains, others fanning out into the depths of the coffin like grasping tendrils. It was an impossible sight, a visceral confirmation of their darkest fears. This wasn't just a grave; it was a nexus, a point of origin for the horror that had stalked their small town, a horror they had inadvertently unleashed.

Hannah forced herself to look, her stomach churning, her breath ragged. Abigail's face, what remained of it, was a gaunt, skeletal mask. Her eyes were gone, leaving hollow, cavernous sockets that seemed to stare into the very core of Hannah's soul. Yet, there was a life in those empty spaces, a furious, ancient sentience that chilled Hannah to the bone. It was Abigail's anger, magnified a thousandfold, a burning resentment that had festered for years, perhaps centuries, waiting for an opportune moment to manifest. The air around the open grave grew heavy, thick with an oppressive energy that pressed down on them, stealing their breath. It was a tangible weight, a spectral shroud woven from Abigail's fury and the dark power that had claimed her.

"She's… she's still here," Emma whispered, her voice a dry rasp. She stumbled back, tripping over a discarded shovelful of earth, her hands flying to her mouth as if to stifle a scream that threatened to erupt. The sound of her fall seemed to awaken something within the coffin, a subtle shift, a rustle of the unnatural hair that made Hannah's skin crawl. It was more than a disturbance of the dead; it was a stirring of the predatory. The very ground beneath them felt unstable, as if the earth itself was a thin veneer over an abyss of unspeakable darkness.

They worked with a frantic, uncoordinated haste, fueled by adrenaline and the lingering terror of the spectral Abigail. The spades, still stained with earth, were resurrected from their discarded positions. They dug with a renewed, grim purpose, not to unearth, but to gather. They needed dry wood. The cemetery offered few readily available resources, mostly damp, decaying branches from ancient oaks, but they scoured the perimeter, pulling fallen limbs, anything that might catch and hold a flame. The air was thick with the unspoken agreement: the faster they worked, the less time they had to dwell on the horror they were about to perpetuate.

Hannah's mind kept replaying the spectral Abigail's lunge, the cold that had seared her hand, the psychic assault that had threatened to shatter her skull. Emma's terrified screams, the feel of those unnaturally strong strands of hair tightening around her ankles—these were vivid, waking nightmares. The thought of that power, that ancient rage, being left unchecked, waiting in the darkness for them, was a constant, gnawing terror. Burning the remains felt like a futile, desperate act of defiance against a force they couldn't possibly comprehend, but it was all they had.

They dragged the splintered wood, the dry leaves they scavenged from sheltered nooks, and anything else that might serve as tinder back to Abigail's grave. The open coffin, stark and terrifying in the dim moonlight, became the macabre centerpiece of their grim undertaking. It was a testament to their transgression, a gaping wound in the earth that they now intended to cauterize with fire.

As they piled the wood, building a rough, uneven pyre around the edges of the open grave, the enormity of what they were doing began to press down on them. This wasn't just a bonfire. This was an attempt to erase a friend, to destroy something unholy that had been born from her corrupted flesh and spirit. Hannah's hands, usually steady, fumbled with the wood, her fingers clumsy and numb. Each piece of wood felt like a betrayal, a confirmation of the finality they were desperately seeking.

Emma, though still visibly shaken, had found a desperate focus in their shared task. She worked with a quiet intensity, her movements precise, as if trying to impose order on the chaos that had erupted in their lives. She arranged the smaller branches meticulously, ensuring a good airflow, her brow furrowed in concentration. Yet, her eyes, when they met Hannah's, held a profound sadness, a mourning for the Abigail they had lost, and for the innocence they had shed that night.

"Do you think… do you think it will work?" Emma's voice was a low murmur, almost a prayer, as she added a final armful of dry leaves to the base of the pyre.

Hannah didn't answer. She didn't know. The rational part of her brain screamed that this was a foolish, childish attempt to fight a supernatural entity with primitive means. But the desperate, terrified part of her clung to the hope that fire, the ultimate purifier, could somehow banish the darkness. It was the only hope they had left.

With the pyre constructed, the next step was the most daunting: igniting it. They had a lighter, a cheap plastic thing they'd "borrowed" from a forgotten camping trip years ago. Hannah fumbled with it, her fingers slick with sweat. The click of the ignition was unnervingly loud in the stillness of the cemetery, and the first few attempts yielded only a weak sputter. The spectral Abigail's laughter seemed to echo in the wind, a cruel mockery of their efforts.

Finally, a small, flickering flame sprang to life. Hannah held it steady, her gaze fixed on the gaping maw of the coffin. It was time. She looked at Emma, who nodded, her face pale but resolute. Together, they approached the grave.

With a deep, steadying breath, Hannah thrust the flame into the tinder at the base of the pyre. The dry leaves caught immediately, a small blaze igniting, licking greedily at the surrounding wood. Emma added her own flame, and soon, a robust fire was crackling, casting dancing shadows across the tombstones. The heat was intense, a welcome sensation against the lingering chill of the grave.

They watched, transfixed, as the flames grew, climbing higher and higher, engulfing the wood. The pyre blazed, a furious beacon in the night, illuminating the skeletal remains within the coffin. The impossibly long hair, still fanned out like a dark halo, seemed to writhe and twist in the heat, an unnatural reaction that made Hannah's stomach clench. It shouldn't have been behaving like that.

The smell of burning wood was quickly joined by another, more sickening aroma. A faint, charring scent, like scorched flesh, began to permeate the air. It was a gruesome perfume, a confirmation that their desperate act was indeed having an effect, or so they desperately hoped. Hannah kept her eyes glued to the coffin, her heart pounding a frantic rhythm against her ribs. She willed the flames to consume everything, to burn away the desecration, the malevolence, the very essence of what Abigail had become.

But as the fire roared, consuming the pyre and, by extension, the remains within the coffin, a chilling realization began to dawn. The spectral Abigail didn't seem to be diminishing. If anything, the flames seemed to feed her, to draw her power. The oppressive energy that had receded momentarily after their encounter now began to return, an even more potent force than before. The air around the grave grew heavy, not with smoke, but with a palpable aura of ancient fury.

The skeletal remains within the coffin began to glow, not with the heat of the fire, but with an inner, infernal luminescence. The dark hair, far from being consumed, seemed to absorb the flames, growing thicker, darker, more vibrant. It writhed and coiled, not with the chaotic energy of burning, but with a controlled, directed power. The moans, which had momentarily subsided, began again, a low, guttural sound that vibrated through the very earth beneath their feet. This wasn't the sound of destruction; it was the sound of augmentation.

Hannah stared, her breath catching in her throat. The fire, their desperate act of purification, was failing. It was a futile gesture, a pathetic attempt to combat a force that operated on a plane far beyond their understanding. The heat of the flames, which had seemed so powerful moments before, now felt insignificant, a mere flicker against the immensity of the darkness they had unleashed. The spectral Abigail's form began to coalesce again within the burning coffin, clearer this time, her eyes burning with an unholy light, her lips curled into a triumphant, contemptuous sneer.

"You think you can destroy me?" the voice echoed, not from the coffin, but from the very air around them, laced with a chilling amusement. "You think fire can cleanse what is bound to the earth, to your own guilt?"

The flames, instead of consuming, were now swirling around the spectral figure, coalescing into a halo of dark, malevolent energy. The long, black hair seemed to weave itself into the flames, becoming an extension of Abigail's spectral form. The skeletal remains within the coffin were no longer visible, consumed not by the fire, but by the burgeoning power of the entity that had taken root there.

"You tried to erase your sin," the voice hissed, the words slithering into their minds like ice. "But you only solidified it. You fed me. You gave me the ritual you so desperately sought."

Hannah's hope, that fragile ember she had clung to, sputtered and died. The pyre, their last desperate measure, had backfired spectacularly. Instead of banishing Abigail, they had inadvertently amplified her power, turning their act of contrition into a catalyst for her even greater resurgence. The futility of their actions washed over her, a crushing wave of despair. They had come to the cemetery seeking closure, and instead, they had gifted their tormentor with a ritual of empowerment.

Emma let out a choked sob beside her, her face a mask of utter devastation. The fire, which had moments ago represented their hope, now seemed a mockery, a symbol of their profound failure. The heat radiating from the coffin was no longer just fire; it was the palpable manifestation of Abigail's amplified rage, a burning, all-consuming fury that promised their utter annihilation.

"This isn't working," Hannah whispered, her voice hollow, her gaze fixed on the infernal glow emanating from the grave. The terror that had been a sharp, piercing stab now settled into a dull, agonizing ache. They had made a terrible mistake. Their attempt to erase their sin had only served to solidify it, to forge it into something even more monstrous. The burning of Abigail's remains, meant to be an act of finality, had become a ritual of her resurrection, a testament to the fact that some horrors, once awakened, could not be so easily extinguished. They had tried to fight the darkness with fire, and the darkness had only grown stronger, fueled by their own desperate, misguided actions. The pyre, intended to be their salvation, was now a monument to their utter and complete failure. The air crackled with an energy that felt both ancient and terrifyingly new, the energy of a power they had not only failed to defeat but had actively helped to create. The futility of their desperate measure hung heavy in the air, as suffocating as the smoke from the dying flames.

The acrid stench of burnt wood and something far more sinister still clung to the air, a tangible miasma that seemed to cling to their very souls. The pyre, meant to be their cleansing fire, was now a smoldering, blackened monument to their catastrophic failure. Embers pulsed with a dying, infernal glow, casting grotesque shadows that danced and writhed like specters themselves across the damp earth. Hannah stared into the still-smoking cavity of the grave, her eyes raw and stinging, not from the smoke, but from the unshed tears of utter, soul-crushing despair. The infernal luminescence that had pulsed from within the coffin had faded, leaving behind only a hollowed-out void that felt, if possible, even more terrifying. It wasn't empty; it was a waiting void, a promise of return.

Emma sat on the cold, damp grass a few feet away, her knees drawn up to her chest, her head buried in her arms. Her shoulders shook with silent, racking sobs, a sound more chilling to Hannah than any scream could have been. It was the sound of a spirit broken, of hope utterly extinguished. Hannah wanted to go to her, to offer some semblance of comfort, but her own limbs felt heavy, leaden, as if anchored to the cursed ground by the sheer weight of their transgression. They had tried to bury a darkness, and in doing so, they had merely dug it a deeper, more fertile grave.

The silence that had fallen after the spectral Abigail's triumphant, mocking pronouncements was the most deafening thing of all. It wasn't the peaceful quiet of a cemetery at rest, but the pregnant, suffocating hush that precedes an even greater storm. The air, which had thrummed with Abigail's amplified power, now felt... heavy. Not with residual energy, but with a kind of watchful stillness. It was the quiet of a predator digesting its meal, of a trap sprung and waiting. Hannah could feel it, a cold, invasive presence that had seeped into the very fabric of the night, into the cemetery, into her. It was a lingering shadow, a whisper of Abigail's continued existence, a testament to the fact that their desperate measures had achieved the exact opposite of their intended purpose.

Hannah's mind reeled, a chaotic mess of images: the impossible length of Abigail's hair, now seemingly woven into the very flames that were supposed to consume it; the skeletal remains, glowing with an unholy light that defied the logic of combustion; the chilling, disembodied voice that had promised their doom. Each memory was a fresh stab of terror, a confirmation of the irreversible error they had made. They hadn't just failed to destroy Abigail; they had, in their desperate ignorance, given her a sacrament. The ritual she had craved, the amplification of her rage, had been gifted to her by their own trembling hands.

"She's... she's still here," Emma whispered, her voice muffled by her arms. It wasn't a question, but a statement of desolate fact.

Hannah couldn't find her voice. She simply nodded, her gaze fixed on the blackened earth. The feeling was undeniable. Abigail's presence wasn't a memory; it was an active, lingering influence. It was a cold knot in Hannah's stomach, a prickling sensation on her skin, a suffocating pressure in her chest. It was the palpable certainty that even though the fire had died down, the entity it was meant to destroy had not. It had merely retreated, regrouped, and was now observing them, toying with them, perhaps even savoring their despair.

They had unearthed a horror, and then, in a twisted act of misguided atonement, they had tried to erase it with fire. It was a primitive, desperate attempt to combat an ancient, malignant force. And it had failed. Utterly. Catastrophically failed. The specter's words echoed in Hannah's mind: "You tried to erase your sin. But you only solidified it. You fed me. You gave me the ritual you so desperately sought." The truth of it was a bitter, burning acid in her throat.

The sheer exhaustion was overwhelming. It wasn't just physical; it was an exhaustion of the spirit. Every nerve ending felt frayed, every cell in her body screamed in protest. The adrenaline that had fueled their frantic actions had long since dissipated, leaving behind a hollowed-out shell of a person. Hannah felt like a plucked string, vibrating with a residual dread that would never fully cease. They had walked into the cemetery seeking to confront and neutralize a threat, and they had walked out having empowered it, having woven themselves into its terrible tapestry.

Hannah looked at the scattered remnants of the pyre—the charred wood, the scattered ashes, the gaping, disturbed earth. It was a scene of devastation, a testament to their futility. The night, which had felt oppressive before, now felt malevolent. The wind rustling through the trees sounded like hushed whispers, like laughter, like the drawn-out sigh of a satisfied entity. It was a mocking symphony, played out just for them.

"What do we do now?" Emma finally managed to croak, her voice raw and broken. She slowly lifted her head, her face streaked with dirt and tears, her eyes wide and haunted. The innocent spark that had once resided there had been replaced by a deep, pervasive terror.

Hannah wished she had an answer. The certainty that had guided their desperate actions—the belief that burning the remains would end it—was gone. It had been replaced by a gnawing uncertainty, a terrifying realization that they were in far over their heads. They had ventured into forbidden territory, disturbed something ancient and vengeful, and now they were paying the price. And it wasn't just about appeasing Abigail's restless spirit anymore. It was about survival.

The lingering shadow of Abigail, now amplified and emboldened, felt like a tangible weight pressing down on them. It was a cold, unyielding pressure that promised no respite. They were no longer simply dealing with the aftermath of a terrifying encounter; they were in the direct aftermath of having created something far worse. The consequences of their actions were not confined to the cemetery, or to that night. They were imprinted upon them, a brand of fear and guilt that would follow them wherever they went.

Hannah stood up, her muscles protesting with every movement. She needed to get Emma out of here, away from this cursed place. But even as she reached out a hand to her friend, she knew there was no escape. Abigail's shadow wasn't just in the cemetery; it was in their memories, in their fear, and now, it was irrevocably intertwined with their very beings. They had tried to banish a demon, and they had succeeded only in forging it anew. The lingering shadow of their failure was far more terrifying than the spectral presence itself, for it promised a slow, agonizing descent into a darkness they had unwittingly helped to create.

Their desperate measures had not brought an end, but a horrifying beginning. The exhaustion was profound, a deep weariness that seeped into their bones, but the terror was even deeper, a primal fear of what they had unleashed and the chilling certainty that it was not yet finished with them. The silence of the cemetery was not a sign of peace, but a chilling promise of what was to come.

Chapter 6:
The Unending Nightmare

The oppressive stillness of the cemetery had begun to recede, not with the dawn, but with the slow, insidious creep of denial. Hannah found herself clinging to the fragments of that desperate hope like a drowning swimmer clinging to a piece of driftwood.

They had done something. They had performed a ritual, however flawed, however incomplete. Abigail's spectral form had been undeniably weakened, her chilling pronouncements laced with a desperation that hadn't been present before. The light that had emanated from her grave had flickered, sputtered, and died, unlike its previous infernal luminescence. Perhaps, just perhaps, the fire had been enough.

Perhaps the disturbance of her resting place, the very act of confronting her physical form, had disrupted whatever unholy tether held her to this world. It was a fragile thought, a delicate butterfly's wing against the howling gale of their recent trauma, but Hannah latched onto it with the fierce grip of someone desperate to believe in anything other than utter, unending damnation.

Emma, too, seemed to be latching onto this fragile hope. The catatonic silence that had followed their retreat from the cemetery had gradually given way to a tentative, almost fearful, resumption of activity. They had driven back in strained silence, the car's headlights cutting sterile swathes through the inky blackness, the only sound the dull thud of the tires on the asphalt. Back in the relative safety of Hannah's small apartment, a fragile normalcy began to assert itself. They made tea, the clinking of mugs a surprisingly comforting sound in the echoing silence. They didn't speak of what had happened, not directly, but the unspoken understanding hung heavy in the air, a shared secret that bound them tighter than any spoken vow. They were survivors. They had faced the abyss and, in some terrifying, incomprehensible way, managed to pull back from the brink.

In the days that followed, a strange sort of routine began to reassert itself, albeit a deeply fractured one. Hannah went to work, her mind a blurry landscape of spreadsheets and customer service calls, each mundane task a deliberate attempt to anchor herself to the solid ground of the ordinary. She tried to focus on the rhythm of her days, on the predictable progression of hours, on the comforting banality of everyday life. She would catch herself staring out the window, her gaze distant, and then force herself to blink, to refocus on the task at hand, to push away the encroaching tendrils of memory. The gnawing anxiety was still there, a persistent hum beneath the surface of her awareness, but it was manageable. It was a shadow, not a suffocating presence. She reasoned that this must be what it felt like to survive a terrible ordeal, to emerge from the crucible bearing the scars but not the complete destruction.

Emma tried to do the same. She attempted to re-engage with her art, setting up her easel in her small studio apartment, the familiar smell of turpentine and oil paint a welcome distraction. She would spend hours there, her brow furrowed in concentration, her hands stained with pigment. Sometimes, a flicker of her old passion would ignite, a moment where the canvas seemed to come alive under her brushstrokes, where the world outside the studio faded into insignificance. These were the moments Hannah clung to, the evidence that the light within Emma had not been extinguished, merely dimmed. They would talk on the phone, their conversations carefully curated, devoid of any mention of the cemetery, of the pyre, of the spectral Abigail. They spoke of mundane things: new art supplies, upcoming exhibitions, the annoying neighbor's dog. It was a conscious, collective effort to pretend that the nightmare had passed, that the darkness they had encountered had been vanquished.

This period of deceptive calm, however, was not born of genuine peace, but of a desperate, shared desire to believe in a reprieve. It was the quiet before the storm, the moment of suspended breath when one almost believes that the danger has passed. Hannah found herself scrutinizing every flicker of light, every creak of the floorboards, every rustle of leaves outside her window. She'd wake in the night with a gasp, her heart hammering against her ribs, convinced she heard the whisper of Abigail's name on the wind, or saw a fleeting shadow dart across the edge of her vision. These moments of heightened anxiety, however, were usually followed by a wave of self-recrimination. She was letting the trauma get the better of her, she told herself. They had done all they could. Abigail was gone.

Emma experienced similar bouts of paranoia. She would find herself staring at her own reflection in mirrors, half-expecting to see Abigail's gaunt, spectral face superimposed over her own. She started leaving lights on all night, the constant hum of electricity a fragile bulwark against the encroaching darkness. Her art, which had once been her sanctuary, now sometimes felt like a taunt. She'd be painting a serene landscape, only to find her hand instinctively adding a grotesque, twisted branch, or a pair of malevolent eyes peering from the shadows of the trees. She would then quickly paint over it, her breath coming in shallow gasps, trying to erase the involuntary intrusion of the nightmare into her art.

Despite these lingering anxieties, they both desperately clung to the illusion of normalcy. They had to. To acknowledge the true depth of their failure, the terrifying amplification of Abigail's power, was to invite a despair so profound it threatened to consume them entirely. They convinced themselves that the spectral Abigail they had seen had been a manifestation of their fear, a distorted echo of the lingering energy in the cemetery. The fact that the pyre had been extinguished, that the earth had been disturbed, that they had actively confronted the source of their terror – these were tangible actions, proofs of their agency. They had taken action, and action, however imperfect, was better than passive surrender.

Hannah remembered a particular evening, about a week after the disastrous ritual. She and Emma had decided to go out for dinner, a deliberate attempt to reclaim a sliver of their pre-Abigail lives. They chose a bustling Italian restaurant, the air thick with the aroma of garlic and basil, the cacophony of happy chatter a welcome balm to their frayed nerves. For the first hour, it felt almost normal. They laughed at silly jokes, reminisced about college days, and even managed to enjoy their meals. Hannah allowed herself to relax, a genuine smile gracing her lips. She dared to believe that perhaps, just perhaps, this was it: the end of the nightmare, the beginning of healing.

Then, as they were finishing their tiramisu, Hannah's gaze drifted towards the large window that overlooked the street. A young woman, dressed in a pale, almost ethereal white dress, was walking by. It was a common sight in the city, a simple passerby. But as the woman turned her head slightly, her dark hair falling across her cheek, Hannah's breath hitched. For a fleeting, terrifying instant, the woman's profile, the unnatural stillness of her posture, the unsettling paleness of her skin, all coalesced into a horrifyingly familiar image. It was Abigail. Or rather, a ghost of Abigail, a phantom conjured by Hannah's own tormented mind. The image was so vivid, so visceral, that Hannah felt a cold dread wash over her. She blinked, and the woman was gone, replaced by the ordinary flow of pedestrian traffic.

She looked at Emma, who was reaching for her water glass. Her friend's expression was serene, her eyes bright with the lingering warmth of their shared meal. She hadn't seen it. Or, if she had, she hadn't recognized it. Hannah's heart pounded a frantic rhythm against her ribs. Was she losing her mind? Was this the inevitable consequence of what they had done? The moment of false hope, so comforting just moments before, shattered like glass, leaving behind jagged shards of terror.

"You okay?" Emma asked, her brow furrowed slightly. "You just went… quiet."

Hannah forced a smile, her voice betraying none of the panic that was clawing at her throat. "Yeah. Just… thinking about that awful smell from the cemetery. It's still in my head, I think." It was a weak excuse, but it was all she had.

Emma nodded, her expression sympathetic. "I know. Me too. But it will fade, Hannah. It has to."

Hannah wanted to believe her. She truly did. But as she looked at Emma, at the faint tremor in her hand as she lifted her glass, she saw a reflection of her own fear, a subtle crack in the facade of normalcy. The quiet, the carefully constructed normalcy, was just that—a fragile illusion. The specter of Abigail, whether real or imagined, was already beginning to weave its way back into their lives, a chilling reminder that the pyre had not been an ending, but a horrific, unforgivable prelude. The peace they were desperately trying to cultivate was a lie, a temporary truce in a war they had already lost. The fear, long dormant, began to stir, whispering insidious doubts that eroded the flimsy walls of their composure. This was not a time of healing; it was a time of agonizing, drawn-out torment, where the deepest wounds were not the physical ones, but the ones etched onto their souls.

The deceptive calm, the carefully curated normalcy Hannah and Emma had so desperately clung to, began to unravel not with a bang, but with an unnerving, profound silence. It started innocuously—a missed text, an unanswered phone call. Hannah, still trapped in the exhausting cycle of pretending, initially attributed it to Emma losing herself in her art, a common enough occurrence. Perhaps she'd been so absorbed in a new canvas that her phone had simply been forgotten, silenced amidst the turpentine fumes and the rustle of charcoal. But as the hours stretched, a prickle of unease, a familiar tremor of dread, began to slither its way up Hannah's spine.

She tried calling again. Voicemail. The same automated, cheerful voice that usually filled Hannah with a mild annoyance now sent a jolt of cold fear through her. Emma never let her calls go to voicemail. Not when Hannah was the only person she had left to truly confide in, the only one who understood the suffocating weight of their shared trauma. Hannah's mind, already a battlefield of suppressed memories and anxious projections, began to conjure terrifying scenarios with alarming speed. Had Abigail returned, more insidious and cunning than before? Had she somehow lured Emma away, her spectral tendrils reaching into their fragile reality once more?

Panic, cold and sharp, began to assert itself. Hannah abandoned her work, the sterile office environment suddenly feeling like a cage. She practically ran out, her sensible heels clattering on the pavement, her breath coming in ragged gasps. She hailed a cab, her voice tight with a desperate urgency as she gave Emma's address. Every moment felt like an eternity, each traffic light an agonizing delay. The city, usually a vibrant tapestry of life, seemed to press in on her, its noise and motion a mocking counterpoint to the growing emptiness inside her.

Arriving at Emma's apartment building, Hannah's heart hammered against her ribs with a frantic, unsteady rhythm. She burst through the main door, not bothering to ring the bell, and raced up the stairs, her footsteps echoing the desperate pounding in her chest. She reached Emma's apartment, fumbling with the keys she kept for emergencies, her fingers trembling so violently she could barely insert the key into the lock.

The door swung open to reveal… nothing. Or rather, an emptiness that screamed louder than any noise. The apartment was undisturbed, eerily tidy. Her easel stood in the corner, a half-finished landscape bathed in the pale afternoon light, the vibrant colors mocking the desolation of the room. A mug of what looked like cold tea sat on a small table beside a sketchbook, its pages open to a charcoal drawing of a wilting rose. Everything was precisely as Emma might have left it if she had simply stepped out for a moment. But the silence—the profound, absolute silence—was wrong. It felt heavy, pregnant with absence.

Hannah called Emma's name, her voice a fragile thread in the suffocating quiet. "Emma? Emma, are you here?" Her words were swallowed by the room, no answer returning but the frantic beating of her own heart. She moved through the small apartment, her eyes scanning every corner, her breath catching in her throat. The bedroom was neat, the bed made. The bathroom was empty, the shower curtain drawn. There was no sign of a struggle, no note, nothing to suggest that Emma had left willingly, or that she had been forcibly taken. It was as if she had simply… evaporated.

The initial wave of panic began to subside, replaced by a chilling, creeping despair. Her worst fears, the ones she had tried so hard to suppress, were solidifying into a terrifying reality. Abigail had not been vanquished. The pyre, the ritual, the supposed disruption of her spectral hold—it had all been a futile gesture. Abigail had merely been waiting, her malevolent gaze fixed on them, picking her moment. And she had chosen Emma.

Hannah sank onto the sofa, the plush cushions offering no comfort, only a stark reminder of Emma's presence, now violently erased. Tears, hot and bitter, welled in her eyes and spilled down her cheeks. She was alone. Utterly, terrifyingly alone. The shared burden, the fragile alliance that had sustained her through the darkest hours, was gone. Emma, her anchor, her confidante, her only true friend in this escalating nightmare, had been ripped away.

The thought sent another jolt of pure terror through her. If Abigail had taken Emma, what did that mean for her? Was she next? Had Abigail simply moved on to her primary target, leaving Hannah to witness the final act of her descent into madness? The isolation was crushing. There was no one to turn to, no one to validate her terror, no one to share the crushing weight of what had happened. The emptiness in the apartment was a reflection of the void that had opened up in Hannah's life, a gaping wound that threatened to consume her.

She forced herself to stand, a primal urge to do something, anything, overriding the crushing despair. She needed to search, to look for clues, to find some trace of where Emma had gone. She retraced Emma's steps through the apartment, her gaze sharp, searching for anything out of the ordinary. She examined the sketchbook, the charcoal drawing of the wilting rose suddenly imbued with a deeper, more sinister meaning. Was it a premonition? A reflection of Emma's own fading hope, her wilting spirit under Abigail's influence?

She picked up the discarded tea mug, a faint imprint of Emma's lips still visible on the rim. It was a small, tangible link to her friend, a heartbreaking reminder of the normalcy they had been so close to reclaiming. Hannah's hand trembled as she brought it to her lips, a desperate, foolish gesture, as if she could absorb some residual essence of Emma. The tea was cold, bitter, tasting of nothing but despair.

Her eyes landed on the window, and for a terrifying moment, she saw it again. A flicker in the periphery, a pale, indistinct shape against the darkening sky. She didn't dare look directly, her blood freezing in her veins. It was Abigail. She knew it with a certainty that chilled her to the bone. Abigail was out there, watching, savoring her victory. And she had taken Emma. The thought was a physical blow, knocking the wind out of Hannah.

She stumbled back from the window, her breath coming in ragged gasps. The carefully constructed walls of her sanity, already weakened by weeks of terror, were crumbling at an alarming rate. She was alone, hunted, and the one person who understood had been taken. The silence of the apartment was no longer just an absence of noise; it was a suffocating presence, the palpable silence of death, of finality.

Hannah's mind raced, trying to piece together the fragmented events, to find logic in the madness. The cemetery, the ritual, Abigail's weakened state… it had all been a lie. A cruel trick of Abigail's power, a momentary lull before the true onslaught. They had thought they had gained a reprieve, but they had only been lulled into a false sense of security. Abigail had been playing a much longer, much crueler game.

She collapsed onto the floor, her body wracked with sobs. The world had shrunk to this small, silent apartment, filled with the ghost of her best friend. She was trapped in a nightmare from which there was no waking. The city outside, with its oblivious inhabitants, felt a million miles away. Her phone lay on the floor beside her, silent and useless. There was no one to call, no one to help.

The sheer, unadulterated terror of her isolation washed over her, threatening to drown her. She was the last one. The sole survivor. The ultimate target. Abigail had systematically eliminated anyone who had stood in her way, anyone who had dared to challenge her. First Mark, then the others who had been drawn into their orbit, and now Emma. And Hannah knew, with a chilling certainty that settled deep in her bones, that Abigail wasn't finished. The true nightmare was only just beginning, and she was at its epicenter, utterly alone and exposed. The absence of Emma was not just a personal tragedy; it was a stark, terrifying declaration of Abigail's ultimate victory, a prelude to Hannah's own inevitable, horrifying end. The emptiness where Emma had stood was a gaping void, a testament to the power of the darkness that had consumed her friend, and that now waited, patiently, for Hannah.

The key turned in the lock with a click that sounded impossibly loud in the stifling silence of her own apartment. Hannah's apartment. Her sanctuary, or what was left of it. She'd fled Emma's empty, echoing space, the tangible proof of her friend's horrifying absence a weight she could no longer bear. Now, the familiar scent of her own home, a mix of lavender and old paperbacks, offered no comfort. It was tainted, permeated by the encroaching dread that had become her constant companion. She closed the door, the latch securing with a definitive thud, a futile attempt to barricade herself against an enemy that didn't need doors or windows.

She leaned against the cool wood, her breath hitching. The events of the past few hours, the desperate search, the soul-crushing discovery of Emma's complete vanishing, had left her drained, her nerves frayed to the point of breaking. The city outside, a cacophony of indifferent life, seemed to mock her isolation. She was adrift, a lone vessel in a tempest, and the storm was closing in. She forced herself to move, to go through the motions. Make tea. Turn on the lights. Anything to push back the encroaching darkness that threatened to engulf her entirely. But even the mundane actions felt hollow, the bright glare of the lamps doing little to dispel the shadows that seemed to gather in the corners of her vision.

As she made her way to the kitchen, a subtle shift in the atmosphere pricked at her senses. It was a familiar sensation, one that had become intimately, terrifyingly ingrained in her consciousness. The air, moments before still and unremarkable, began to grow heavy, charged with an unseen energy. A profound, unnatural cold seeped into the room, raising gooseflesh on her arms despite the warmth of her sweater. It wasn't the chill of an open window or a faulty heater. This was a cold that emanated from within, a spectral frost that bypassed her skin and settled deep into her bones.

She paused, her hand hovering over the kettle. Her heart began to thud against her ribs, a frantic, erratic beat against the backdrop of the growing silence. The usual hum of the refrigerator seemed to fade, replaced by a low, almost imperceptible vibration that seemed to resonate within her very skull. It was the prelude. The unmistakable overture to Abigail's presence. She had hoped, desperately, that by returning to her own space, she might have outrun it, or at least put some distance between herself and the entity that had stolen Emma. But it was a foolish hope, a denial of the grim reality. Abigail was not bound by physical space. Abigail was an echo, a stain, a parasitic consciousness that latched onto the minds and souls of the living.

A faint rustling sound, like dry leaves skittering across a barren floor, brushed against her ears. Hannah's eyes darted around the living room, her gaze snagging on the shifting patterns of light and shadow cast by the streetlamps outside. Nothing. It was always nothing, at first. The subtle manipulations, the insidious build-up of unease, the psychological warfare that preceded the overt manifestations. Abigail was a predator, and she liked to toy with her prey.

She gripped the edge of the counter, her knuckles white. The cold intensified, and with it, a sense of profound dread washed over her. It was more than just fear; it was a primal terror, an instinctual recognition of an encroaching evil that promised annihilation. She could feel it now, a tangible pressure in the air, a suffocating weight that made it difficult to breathe. It was as if the very essence of the room was being distorted, warped by an unseen malevolence.

Then came the whispers.

Faint at first, like the murmur of distant voices carried on the wind, they began to weave their way into her consciousness. They were indistinct, fragmented, yet laced with a familiar venom. Hannah strained to decipher them, her mind a battlefield of terror and desperate attempts at rationality. Were they actual words, or the fevered imaginings of her own fractured psyche? The line between reality and delusion had blurred so many times before that she could no longer trust her own perceptions.

"…so alone…"

The whisper seemed to coil around her, a venomous caress. It was a dark echo of her own despair, twisted and amplified by Abigail's insidious influence. Hannah squeezed her eyes shut, trying to block out the insidious intrusion. She couldn't let it in. Not now. Not when Emma was gone.

"…weak… fragile…"

The words slithered into her mind, each syllable laced with icy contempt. They targeted her deepest insecurities, the raw wounds left by years of trauma, and the recent, devastating loss of her friend. Abigail knew her vulnerabilities, her breaking points, and she was exploiting them with ruthless precision. Hannah's breath hitched, a sob threatening to escape her throat. She wanted to scream, to rage against the unseen tormentor, but her voice was trapped, choked by a fear so profound it rendered her mute.

She felt a subtle movement to her left, a disturbance in the air that suggested a presence had just shifted, had just glided past her. She flinched, her body tensing, ready to bolt, though she knew there was nowhere to run. Abigail wasn't an entity that could be outrun. She was a concept, a manifestation of the darkness that festered within the world, and now, within Hannah's own life.

Her gaze swept across the room again, her eyes wide, searching for any visual confirmation of the unseen horror. The familiar objects of her apartment – the worn armchair, the overflowing bookshelf, the framed photographs of happier times – seemed to warp and distort in her peripheral vision. The shadows deepened, coalescing into indistinct shapes that writhed and shifted, playing tricks on her already strained senses.

A faint, dry scratching sound emanated from the wall beside her. It was a sound like fingernails dragging across plaster, slow and deliberate. Hannah recoiled, her hand flying to her mouth to stifle a scream. The sound wasn't just external; it felt as if it were emanating from within the walls, from the very fabric of her home. Abigail was here. Not just in the apartment, but in it. Seeping into its foundations, claiming it as her own.

The cold was no longer just a sensation; it was a palpable presence, an icy hand reaching out to grasp her. It coiled around her, squeezing the warmth from her body, the very air she breathed. It was the touch of death, the chilling embrace of the abyss. Hannah whimpered, her knees buckling slightly. She felt an overwhelming urge to curl into a ball, to make herself small, invisible, hoping that by ceasing to exist, she might escape the entity's attention.

But Abigail wasn't content with invisibility. The whispers grew louder, more distinct, coalescing into a single, malevolent voice that seemed to emanate from every direction at once. It was a voice that had once been familiar, yet now it was utterly alien, twisted by an ancient, unspeakable hatred.

"Hannah."

The single word, spoken in a voice that was both a caress and a threat, pierced through the fog of Hannah's fear. It was Abigail. There was no mistaking it. The sibilant hiss, the underlying current of triumph and cruelty – it was all there. And it was directed at her.

Hannah's eyes snapped open, her gaze fixed on a point in the center of the room. The air there seemed to shimmer, to warp, as if looking through heat haze. Slowly, agonizingly, a form began to coalesce. It was indistinct at first, a swirling vortex of shadow and distorted light. But as it gained substance, Hannah's blood ran colder than the spectral chill that permeated the room.

It was Abigail.

Not the wraith-like apparition she remembered from the cemetery, nor the fleeting glimpses she'd caught in her periphery. This was something more solid, more terrifyingly present. Abigail stood before her, a figure composed of pure darkness, her form shifting and coalescing like smoke. Yet, within the shifting shadows, Hannah could discern features: the gauntness of her face, the hollow sockets where eyes should have been, now glowing with an inner, malevolent light. Her mouth, a thin, cruel line, stretched into a smile that promised infinite torment.

The whispers ceased, replaced by a chilling, guttural sound that might have been a laugh. It was a sound that promised the unmaking of all things, the unraveling of reality itself. Hannah could feel her own sanity fraying at the edges, the carefully constructed defenses she had erected over the years crumbling under the sheer force of Abigail's presence.

"You thought you could escape me?" Abigail's voice was a rasping whisper, each syllable dripping with venom. "You thought that little charade in the cemetery would suffice?"

Hannah wanted to respond, to deny, to fight back, but her body refused to cooperate. She was paralyzed by a terror so profound it had seized every muscle, every nerve ending. All she could do was stare, her eyes wide with horror, as Abigail took a slow, deliberate step towards her.

The spectral cold intensified, biting at Hannah's exposed skin. The very air seemed to crackle with energy, the darkness emanating from Abigail's form expanding, reaching out like tendrils of shadow. It wasn't just a presence anymore; it was an overwhelming, inescapable force that had come to claim her.

"Emma was a distraction," Abigail hissed, her voice echoing with a chilling resonance that seemed to vibrate through the floorboards. "A weakness. And now," her shadowy form seemed to swell, her glowing eyes fixed solely on Hannah, "she is gone. And you, Hannah, are mine."

The words were a death knell, a pronouncement of doom. Hannah's world narrowed to the terrifying figure before her. The carefully maintained normalcy of her apartment had been shattered, replaced by the stark, horrifying reality of Abigail's return. She was trapped. Hunted.

And this time, there was no escape. The nightmare had returned, not as a phantom threat, but as a monstrous, undeniable reality, standing directly in front of her, ready to devour her whole. The sheer power radiating from Abigail was suffocating, a palpable wave of dark energy that pressed in on Hannah, threatening to crush her. She could feel the tendrils of Abigail's influence probing at the edges of her consciousness, seeking to unravel the remaining threads of her sanity. It was an overwhelming onslaught, designed to break her completely.

Abigail moved closer, her shadowy form seeming to absorb the very light from the room, casting deeper, more menacing shadows. The air grew colder still, so cold that Hannah's breath plumed in front of her. She could feel the cold seeping into her bones, a chilling premonition of the oblivion that awaited her.

Abigail's lips, a thin slash of darkness, curled into a semblance of a smile, revealing a glimpse of impossibly sharp, shadowed teeth. The sight was enough to make Hannah's stomach churn with revulsion and terror. This was not merely a haunting; this was a predatory advance, a consummation of a terrible hunger that had been building for years. The realization that Emma's disappearance was not an end, but a stepping stone for Abigail's ultimate goal, sent a fresh wave of icy dread through Hannah. She had underestimated the entity, had placed too much faith in their desperate ritual, and now the consequences were devastatingly clear.

"You fought so hard," Abigail continued, her voice a low, seductive murmur that carried an undertone of pure malice. "You thought you had won. Such a touching display of defiance. But defiance only makes the surrender all the sweeter." She reached out a hand, a limb formed of swirling darkness, and slowly, deliberately, traced the outline of Hannah's face in the air, never actually touching her. Yet, Hannah felt a phantom sensation, an icy caress that sent shivers down her spine. It was a violation, a spiritual trespass that left her feeling exposed and utterly vulnerable.

The room seemed to spin, the familiar surroundings of her apartment twisting and distorting as Abigail's power exerted its influence. The walls appeared to breathe, to warp inwards, and the very air felt thick with an invisible, suffocating presence.

Hannah stumbled back, her hand flying out to steady herself against a nearby table, sending a stack of books tumbling to the floor with a series of dull thuds. The noise, normally insignificant, now seemed deafening in the charged silence that followed. It was a momentary distraction, a ripple in the suffocating stillness that Abigail had imposed upon the space.

Abigail's gaze, burning with an unholy light, followed her movement, her smile widening. "No need to panic, Hannah," she crooned, her voice laced with a mocking tenderness. "This is not an ending. It is merely a transition. A reclaiming." Her shadowy hand continued its slow, deliberate sweep, moving down Hannah's body as if appraising a prize. Hannah flinched with each movement, her skin crawling at the phantom touch. It was a violation that went beyond the physical, probing at the deepest recesses of her being.

"You see," Abigail whispered, her voice growing slightly louder, carrying a distinct note of triumph, "your grief… your despair… it is a powerful fuel. And you have so much of it now, don't you?" A faint tremor ran through Hannah as she processed the chilling implication. Abigail was feeding on her anguish, her profound sorrow over Emma's disappearance. Every tear shed, every pang of guilt, every moment of paralyzing fear, was directly empowering the entity. The thought was a fresh wave of horror, adding another layer to the already unbearable weight of her suffering.

Hannah's breath came in short, ragged gasps. She felt a desperate need to fight, to resist, to find some flicker of defiance within the suffocating despair. But the sheer overwhelming nature of Abigail's presence, the palpable aura of ancient evil that radiated from her, threatened to extinguish any spark of hope. She was a creature of pure darkness, a force of destruction that fed on the very essence of life and light.

And Hannah, stripped of her friend and her courage, felt utterly powerless against her. The fear was a physical entity, constricting her chest, making it impossible to draw a full breath. Her mind reeled, struggling to comprehend the magnitude of the horror that had descended upon her. This was not a continuation of the nightmare; this was its terrifying, undeniable climax. Abigail's form pulsed with dark energy, the shadows swirling and intensifying, as if the very air was being consumed by her malevolent presence. Hannah could feel the tendrils of her influence reaching deeper, probing at the very core of her being, seeking to unravel her from the inside out. The cold was no longer just an external sensation; it was a chilling embrace that threatened to freeze her soul.

Her gaze was locked onto the space where Abigail had appeared, a place that was now impossibly, terrifyingly occupied. It was no longer a distortion in the air, no longer a suggestion of presence. Abigail was there. Fully, horrifyingly present. Hannah's breath hitched, a ragged, painful sound in the suffocating silence. Her mind, still reeling from the shock of the entity's continued existence and its undeniable relocation to her own apartment, struggled to process the full extent of what stood before her.

The spectral form of Abigail no longer flickered or wavered. It was solid, yet composed of something that defied earthly physics. It was as if the deepest shadows of the night had been woven together, given an impossible, terrifying sentience.

Abigail stood there, a statue carved from despair and malice, her outline sharp against the dim light of Hannah's living room. Her hair, once a vibrant, almost unnaturally lustrous dark brown, now cascaded around her like a storm cloud, each strand seeming to writhe with a life of its own. It wasn't hair as Hannah remembered it; it was a tempest of darkness, crackling with a palpable, unseen energy. The sheer density of the shadow composing it made it seem as though it absorbed the very light that dared to touch it.

And then there were the eyes. Hannah had seen glints of malevolence before, flashes of chilling light that spoke of Abigail's inner torment and rage. But this was different. These weren't eyes; they were twin abysses, burning with an unholy, incandescent fury. They weren't simply glowing; they were beacons of pure, unadulterated hatred, radiating a cold that seeped not just into the room, but into Hannah's very soul. They seemed to bore into Hannah, stripping away every defense, every shred of composure, laying bare the raw, terrified core of her being. The cold wasn't just an external sensation anymore; it was an internal freezing, a paralysis that began in her extremities and crept inwards, stealing her breath, her will, her very ability to react.

Abigail's face, once familiar, now bore the hideous markings of her vengeful transformation. The skin was stretched taut over sharp bone, gaunt and pale, as if drained of all life, yet infused with a supernatural vitality that made her all the more terrifying. The lips, usually a shade of soft rose, were now a thin, bloodless line, pulled back in a perpetual snarl that revealed teeth far too sharp, far too pointed for any living human. It was a rictus of pure, unadulterated rage, a silent scream of eternal damnation made manifest. Her cheeks were hollowed, emphasizing the unnatural sharpness of her cheekbones, and beneath her eyes, dark hollows seemed to deepen into bottomless pits, mirroring the terrifying glow of her gaze.

This was not the Abigail Hannah had known. This was a monstrous perversion, a soul twisted and corrupted by a burning need for retribution. The transformation was complete, horrifyingly so. The gentle, sometimes melancholic friend was gone, replaced by this embodiment of pure, supernatural vengeance. The very air around Abigail seemed to shimmer and warp, a testament to the sheer power she now wielded. It was a power born of betrayal, of agony, and of a desire to inflict suffering that transcended the boundaries of life and death.

Hannah stood frozen, a statue carved from pure, unadulterated terror. Her lungs felt constricted, as if invisible hands were squeezing them shut, preventing her from drawing a breath. Her limbs were leaden, rooted to the spot by a fear so profound it had stolen her capacity for movement. She couldn't scream. The sound was trapped somewhere deep within her throat, a silent wail of utter helplessness. Her eyes were wide, impossibly wide, reflecting the terrifying spectacle before her. She was witnessing the ultimate horror payoff, the terrifying culmination of everything she had feared. Abigail, in her full, terrifying glory, was here, a spectral demon born from grief and rage, and Hannah was its sole, captive audience.

The visual was deeply unsettling, a violation of natural order. Abigail's form pulsed with an almost visible energy, a dark aura that expanded and contracted with her spectral breaths. The shadows within her form shifted and coalesced, creating the illusion of movement even when she stood still, as if the very essence of her being was in constant, terrifying flux. The details of her visage were etched into Hannah's memory with a clarity that was both horrifying and absolute. The way the fabric of her spectral dress seemed to flow like liquid night, clinging to her form yet somehow insubstantial. The way the air around her was visibly colder, misting slightly with each spectral exhalation. It was a terrifying tableau, a nightmare made flesh, or rather, made shadow.

Abigail took a slow, deliberate step forward. The sound of her movement was not a footfall, but a subtle displacement of the charged air, a whisper of displaced energy that seemed to echo in Hannah's bones. Each step brought her closer, and with each step, the oppressive weight of her presence grew. Hannah could feel the primal instinct to flee screaming within her, a desperate, animalistic urge to escape this monstrous entity. But her body remained a prisoner of her terror, unresponsive to her desperate mental commands. She was utterly exposed, a lamb before a wolf, and the wolf was a supernatural entity of unimaginable power and wrath.

The details of Abigail's face were now so clear, so horrifically distinct, that Hannah could discern the subtle contortions of her spectral features. A faint tremor ran through Abigail's jaw, a visible manifestation of the consuming rage that fueled her. Her brow was furrowed, not in sadness, but in a deep, abiding fury that seemed to have carved permanent lines of hatred into her ethereal flesh. The glow in her eyes intensified as she focused her unholy gaze directly upon Hannah, and for a fleeting, agonizing moment, Hannah felt as if her very essence was being scoured, probed, and judged by this spectral arbiter of torment.

The realization that this was the culmination of all the dread, all the fear, all the agonizing uncertainty, struck Hannah with a force that was almost physical. This was not just a haunting; this was an indictment. Abigail had come for her, not just to torment, but to consume, to obliterate the one person she deemed responsible for her eternal suffering. The meticulous crafting of Abigail's terrifying visage served a singular purpose: to break Hannah completely, to reduce her to a state of utter, abject terror before the final annihilation. And it was working. Every detail, from the swirling vortex of her hair to the icy flames in her eyes, was designed to inflict maximum psychological damage, to ensure that Hannah's final moments were filled with the absolute, soul-shattering horror of facing her tormentor in her full, terrifying might. Hannah could feel her sanity fraying at the edges, the carefully constructed walls of her mind crumbling under the sheer, overwhelming pressure of Abigail's supernatural presence. This was the climax of the unending nightmare, and it was more terrifying than she could have ever imagined.

Abigail's presence was a palpable force, a suffocating shroud of cold and dread that pressed in on Hannah from all sides. The sheer intensity of the spectral power radiating from her was enough to make the air crackle, to make the very foundations of the apartment groan under an unseen strain. It was a power honed by years of torment, by a burning resentment that had festered and grown until it had consumed Abigail's very being. Now, that power was focused, honed to a razor's edge, and directed with absolute precision at Hannah.

The visual details of Abigail's transformation were not subtle; they were overtly horrific, designed to instill a primal, visceral fear. Her skin seemed to stretch unnaturally thin, revealing glimpses of what lay beneath the spectral surface—a swirling darkness, a chaotic void that hinted at the unimaginable depths of her suffering and rage. The spectral fabric of her clothing seemed to shift and ripple, not like cloth caught in a breeze, but like living shadows contorting and reforming, constantly mirroring the turmoil within her.

As Abigail continued her slow, deliberate advance, Hannah felt her own body begin to tremble uncontrollably. It wasn't a tremor of fear alone; it was a deep, cellular reaction to the raw, unbridled power that was now mere feet away. The spectral cold intensified, biting at her exposed skin, stealing the warmth from her limbs. Her breath came in shallow, desperate gasps, each inhalation a struggle against the suffocating density of Abigail's aura. The silence in the room was profound, a heavy, unnatural stillness broken only by the frantic hammering of Hannah's own heart against her ribs.

Abigail's burning eyes fixed on Hannah's face, and a chilling, humorless smile stretched her thin, spectral lips. It was a smile that promised pain, a grimace of pure, unadulterated malevolence. In that smile, Hannah saw not just rage, but a deep, unquenchable thirst for retribution, a hunger that had been building for an eternity. The vengeful spirit was no longer a fleeting glimpse or a whispered threat; she was a tangible, terrifying reality, standing before Hannah in all her horrifying, supernatural glory. The scene was a testament to the full extent of Abigail's vengeful transformation, a stark and terrifying display of the power she wielded against her tormentor. The visual was so potent, so deeply unsettling, that it threatened to shatter Hannah's already fragile hold on reality. She was trapped in the ultimate nightmare, face-to-face with the embodiment of her deepest fears. The sheer horror of Abigail's fully materialized form, the raw power emanating from her, was an overwhelming assault on Hannah's senses. It was a visceral, terrifying spectacle that promised an agonizing end.

The silence that had descended was not a comforting absence of noise, but a heavy, suffocating blanket woven from pure dread. It pressed in on Hannah, stealing the air from her lungs, her heartbeat a frantic, trapped bird against the bars of her ribs.

Abigail's spectral form, a monument to corrupted innocence and unyielding rage, had solidified not just in the room but in Hannah's very psyche. The eyes, those twin abysses of incandescent hatred, bored into Hannah, stripping away the last vestiges of her composure, her will, her very sense of self. This was no longer a haunting; this was an invasion.

"You thought you could silence me," Abigail's voice echoed, not from her lips, but from everywhere at once, a discordant symphony of despair and fury that vibrated through Hannah's bones. It was a voice that had been forged in the fires of betrayal, a sound that carried the weight of a soul ripped asunder and left to fester in eternal torment. Each syllable was laced with a venom that could curdle blood, a chilling testament to the depth of her transformation. Hannah could feel the spectral energy coiling around her, tightening like an unseen noose, constricting her breath, her thoughts.

Hannah's body remained locked in place, a statue carved from sheer terror. Her mind screamed for her to run, to fight, to do something, but her limbs refused to obey. They felt alien, disconnected, heavy as anchors dragging her down into the abyss that was Abigail's presence. She could see the spectral form of Abigail shifting, the shadows that composed her coalescing and swirling, giving the illusion of a predator observing its prey. The details of Abigail's face, the gauntness, the impossibly sharp teeth revealed in a rictus of pure hatred, were burned into Hannah's vision, an indelible scar on her consciousness.

"You took everything from me, Hannah," Abigail continued, her voice weaving through the oppressive silence like a phantom serpent. "My life. My future. My peace." The words were punctuated by the subtle, almost imperceptible vibration of the air around her, a physical manifestation of her immense, unholy power. Hannah could feel the raw energy emanating from Abigail, a cold so profound it seemed to leech the warmth from her very soul. It was a cold that spoke of the grave, of eternal darkness, of a rage that had consumed everything, leaving only the husk of a vengeful spirit.

The spectral figure of Abigail took another step closer, the movement less like walking and more like an inexorable glide, as if propelled by the sheer force of her malice. Hannah could feel her own sanity fraying at the edges, the carefully constructed walls of her mind crumbling under the onslaught of this supernatural terror. Abigail's hair, once a cascade of dark silk, now writhed like a nest of venomous snakes, each strand crackling with an unseen, malevolent energy. It was a horrifyingly beautiful, yet utterly terrifying spectacle, a testament to the complete corruption of what had once been her friend.

"And now," Abigail's voice dropped to a guttural whisper that promised unspeakable horrors, "you will know what it is to suffer. You will know what it is to be consumed. You will know… eternal torment." The final words were drawn out, laced with a chilling finality, a promise that resonated with the crushing weight of unending despair. Hannah felt a scream building within her, a desperate, primal wail of utter helplessness, but it remained trapped, a silent testament to the terror that had rendered her mute.

The spectral form of Abigail seemed to swell, to expand, the shadows within her deepening, intensifying until they threatened to engulf the entire room. Hannah could feel the tendrils of this spectral darkness reaching out, coiling around her, drawing her into the vortex of Abigail's rage. It was a physical sensation, a tightening grip that was both icy and burning, a paradoxical torment that spoke of a power beyond mortal comprehension. The air crackled with an unseen energy, the very fabric of reality seeming to warp and distort around Abigail's spectral form.

Hannah's vision began to blur at the edges, the sharp, terrifying details of Abigail's face momentarily softening, as if the sheer intensity of her presence was overloading Hannah's senses. But then, just as quickly, the clarity returned, sharper, more terrifying than before. Abigail's eyes, those burning abysses of hatred, seemed to grow larger, drawing Hannah in, promising oblivion. The smile on Abigail's lips, that thin, bloodless line pulled back in a perpetual snarl, widened, revealing more of the impossibly sharp teeth, each one a needle of pure malice.

"You are mine now, Hannah," Abigail hissed, the sound a whisper of the damned. "Forever." The words hung in the air, heavy with implication, with the promise of a fate worse than death. Hannah could feel herself weakening, her consciousness slipping, succumbing to the overwhelming power that radiated from her spectral tormentor. The cold intensified, seeping into her very bones, freezing her from the inside out. Her breath hitched, a ragged, dying gasp.

The shadow that was Abigail began to loom larger, closer, her spectral form seeming to press in on Hannah, filling her vision, her mind. Hannah squeezed her eyes shut, a futile attempt to escape the horror, but the image of Abigail's enraged, spectral face was seated behind her eyelids, a permanent fixture in the landscape of her terror. She could feel Abigail's spectral touch, icy fingers brushing against her cheek, sending shivers of pure, unadulterated dread coursing through her. It was a touch that promised not solace, but annihilation.

"This is just the beginning," Abigail whispered, her voice now a chilling caress that promised a symphony of suffering. Hannah could feel the spectral presence beginning to seep into her, to merge with her, to consume her from the inside out. The horror was absolute, the terror a suffocating shroud that left no room for hope, no space for escape. The unending nightmare had reached its terrifying climax, and Hannah was trapped within its suffocating embrace, a willing, or rather, an unwilling participant in her own demise. The last thing she registered before the darkness consumed her was the faint, triumphant smile on Abigail's spectral lips, a promise of an eternity of pain. The air in the room grew impossibly cold, and the silence that followed Abigail's final, chilling pronouncement was absolute, broken only by the phantom echo of Hannah's own silent scream.

Back Matter

- **Poltergeist**: A type of ghost or entity believed to cause physical disturbances, such as loud noises, objects being moved or thrown, and physical attacks.
- **Spectral Manifestation**: The appearance or presence of a ghost or spirit in a visible or tangible form.
- **Psychic Assault**: An attack on an individual's mind or consciousness, often through supernatural or paranormal means.

[Placeholder for relevant folklore or paranormal research texts, e.g., *The Encyclopedia of Ghosts and Spirits* by Thomas Streissguth]

[Placeholder for psychological horror theory or analysis texts, e.g., *The Philosophy of Horror* by Noel Carroll]

www.ingramcontent.com/pod-product-compliance
Lightning Source LLC
Chambersburg PA
CBHW080900030426
42335CB00018B/2413